VEGAN DISHES
FOR SEMI-VEGAN HOUSEHOLDS

kitchen divided

Ellen Jaffe Jones

BOOK PUBLISHING COMPANY
Summertown, Tennessee

Library of Congress Cataloging-in-Publication Data

Jones, Ellen Jaffe.
   Kitchen divided : vegan dishes for semi-vegan households / Ellen Jaffe Jones.
     pages cm
  Includes index.
  ISBN 978-1-57067-292-7 (pbk.) — ISBN 978-1-57067-906-3 (e-book)
 1. Vegan cooking.   I. Title.
  TX837.J5429 2013
  641.5'636—dc23

                               2013000238

Calculations for the nutritional analyses in this book are based on the average number of servings listed with the recipes and the average amount of an ingredient if a range is called for. Calculations are rounded up to the nearest gram. If two options for an ingredient are listed, the first one is used. Not included are optional ingredients and serving suggestions.

Photography: Andrew Schmidt
Food stylists: Barbara Jefferson and Liz Murray
Cover and interior design: John Wincek
Front cover photos and stock photos: 123 RF

Book Publishing Company
PO Box 99
Summertown, TN 38483
888-260-8458
bookpubco.com

ISBN: 978-1-57067-292-7

Printed in Canada

19 18 17 16 15 14 13   1 2 3 4 5 6 7 8 9

Book Publishing Company is a member of Green Press Initiative. We chose to print this title on paper with 100% post consumer recycled content, processed without chlorine, which saves the following natural resources:

    59 trees
    1,861 pounds of solid waste
    27.800 gallons of water
    13,880 pounds of greenhouse gases
    27 million BTU of energy

For more information on Green Press Initiative, visit greenpressinitiative.org.

Environmental impact estimates were made using the Environmental Defense Fund Paper Calculator. For more information, visit papercalculator.org.

Printed on recycled paper

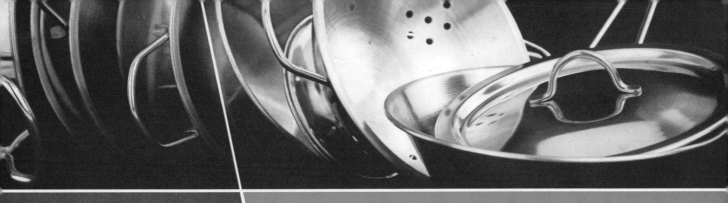

CONTENTS

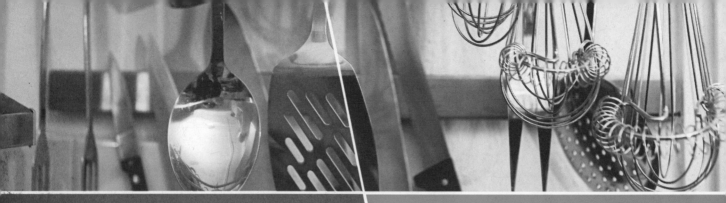

FOREWORD

In a world that seems to be getting more polarized by the day, individuals and families struggle with how to keep peace. Divisive politics, world conflict, and challenging environmental problems strike at the daily decisions we all must make. Eating a plant-based diet can actually reduce conflict on many levels by leading people to a more compassionate attitude toward animals of all kinds and maintaining harmony with the environment.

Ever since former president Bill Clinton went plant-based to save himself from a third heart surgery and, as he said on television, "To be there for the grandkids," the nonvegan world has started to take notice. People can't sign up fast enough for immersion weekends and monthlong challenges to figure out how President Clinton and so many others have regained their health in a relatively short time without all of the drugs and surgeries that doctors usually recommend.

Testimonial after testimonial from people attending vegan cooking classes and weekend health fests attest to the fact that vegan diets are saving lives. Heart disease, cancer, and diabetes are often reversed or even cured in some cases when my patients eat a well-balanced, plant-based diet. While ads for many products are required to have the disclaimer "results are not typical," I have found that for many of my patients on vegan diets, their positive results *are* typical.

Ellen Jaffe Jones was a cooking instructor for Physicians Committee for Responsible Medicine for six years before her first book, *Eat Vegan on $4 a Day,* took off. I recall that one of the many success stories Ellen had in her cooking classes was about a cancer survivor who was diagnosed with multiple myeloma, one of the more fatal forms of bone cancer. The woman had been given an immediate terminal death sentence. After eight months of never counting a calorie, never being hungry, and loving all the plant-based food she was eating, the woman lost 120 pounds and is still alive and well, with good blood test results, almost a decade later.

Ellen's own vegan success story includes losing weight and avoiding the breast cancer, heart disease, diabetes, and Alzheimer's that has struck so many members of her family. She also achieved national recognition as a runner in

races from the 100-meter dash to a marathon; that's quite an accomplishment for an athlete of any age, not to mention someone over sixty.

As an investigative and consumer reporter on television for eighteen years, Ellen won two Emmys and National Press Club awards by exposing crime and corruption, and also uncovering a story that led to an FDA food recall. As a reporter, she covered stories of horrible animal abuse, from puppy mills to animal euthanizing. All of this fueled her passion in her work as a media consultant with our staff. Her experiences eventually led her to do the investigative reporting job of her life: trying to figure out the real truth about the food industry by following the money and special interests surrounding it.

Like many other vegans, Ellen shares her kitchen with a nonvegan spouse. She has had to pick her battles and do the best she could to navigate the social pitfalls that come with living with a family that doesn't share her vegan lifestyle, even when that lifestyle ensures better health. But she knew she had struck a nerve when so many people in her cooking classes would nod in the affirmative when she'd ask, "How many of you live in a mixed marriage?"—a reference to spouses who manage their meals in a divided kitchen. She decided to reach out to everyone who struggles in similar circumstances.

This book is a compilation of Ellen's wit and wisdom on how vegans can coexist with nonvegans in their kitchen. What I love about it is that it doesn't preach. It entices. It will help you prepare vegan meals so tempting, irresistible, and delicious that friends and relatives within smelling range of the kitchen might just dissolve the mixed marriage contract and maybe, just maybe, go vegan once and for all. But if your kitchen partners aren't ready to make the plunge, the recipes here lend themselves to mixing and matching in even the most complicated culinary situations. If you live in a divided kitchen, read on.

Neal Barnard, MD
Physicians Committee for Responsible Medicine (PCRM)

PREFACE

The journey to eating vegan typically starts with a single thought, often about how to improve one's health or lose weight. Eventually, that single thought may become a catalyst leading to many other revelations, or what some describe as a life-altering epiphany. Once people start connecting the dots between what they eat and countless other concerns, such as animal exploitation, environmental degradation, and human health, there's no turning back. For vegans, a powerful incentive to share their realizations with others is common and understandable. But when that mission clashes with the views, preferences, and lifestyle of a partner or family members, conflict is almost inevitable.

My aim with this book is to give you tools that will help you traverse a kitchen divided and maintain peace in your home and relationships. Even if you and your partner or family members never end up on the same page of the menu, so to speak, this book will give you plenty of ideas to streamline your food preparation and meals and simplify your life so you can juggle the demands of cooking for diverse needs. Most importantly, you'll find recipes that will help you get meals on the table in short order, without having to be a short-order cook.

In some households, microwaves have been a solution for divided kitchens. Each person can simply toss a meal in the microwave, nuke it, and be done. But it's expensive to eat processed and packaged foods. Whenever resources are used to get food into a box, bag, can, or jar, the nutritional value of that food goes down and its cost goes up. While microwaved meals are indeed convenient, there are far better alternatives. With the recipes in this book, you'll be able to quickly turn out satisfying home-cooked meals that will appeal to vegans and nonvegans alike, using equipment no fancier than what your grandmother may have used.

Additionally, I want you to have fun in the kitchen. Fun, you ask? Seriously? How could making two or more meals at the same time be fun? Brace yourself to be pleasantly surprised. In this book you'll hear from people who are "living in the trenches" daily and who have developed a wealth of tips for cooking and coping with a divided kitchen. I'll also provide plenty of practical suggestions for how you can avoid the start of World War III and not just survive but thrive in a challenging living situation.

Consider this book a life preserver in the sea of a meat-eating majority. Plus, while you're swimming upstream, you may just end up catching the attention of someone nearby who decides, "I'll have what she's having."

ACKNOWLEDGMENTS

I come from a family of political leaders, business owners, and volunteers who worked for causes because they believed that was the right thing to do. I am so grateful to all of them for many different insights. I owe so much to my mother, who always maintained that patience is a virtue. I needed that advice because I'm the kind of person who wants the world to change *now*.

I can't say enough about all the wonderful people I've had the pleasure of getting to know at Book Publishing Company, which has published some of the most popular vegetarian and vegan books of the past three decades. I had read and used many of them for years without giving much thought to who published them. I spent a year trying to find a publisher for my first book, *Eat Vegan on $4.00 a Day*. Time and again, publishers turned me down because I wasn't already an author or a celebrity—a common vicious cycle for first-time authors to break. But Book Publishing had the guts to say yes, and the rest is history.

Once, while peppering publisher Bob Holzapfel with questions, he answered simply, "Be true to your values. Do not waver. Don't get caught up in today's latest fad." Bob's wife and managing editor at Book Publishing Company, Cynthia Holzapfel, has been a major force in my development as an author. I also feel lucky to have had the guidance of senior editorial director Jo Stepaniak. In my early years as a vegan, I often referred to the many books and cookbooks she's written, never suspecting that some day I'd have the good fortune to work with her. In addition, I've been privileged to get to know other employees at Book Publishing Company who work behind the scenes both in publishing and in organizing vegetarian and vegan food festivals. Huge shout-outs to Andrew, Anna, Barb, Barbara, Dave, John, Liz, Mary Ellen, Thomas, Warren, and everyone who keeps the company ticking. My relationship with Book Publishing

Company originated with Patti Breitman, who worked tirelessly to help me find a publisher for my first book. I send her a thousand thanks.

Major hugs to my friend Roxanne Dinkin, who, after listening to me talk about my wild family history, said, "You know, you ought to write a book about that and maybe include one of your favorite recipes at the end of each chapter." Maybe? Holy guacamole! Little did she know what she had unleashed.

A huge shout-out to my three daughters, who are the pride and joy of my life. I do all of my work with my kids in mind, in the hope that their children may grow up in a world with better health and more favorable environmental odds.

Finally, I owe much to my dear husband, Clarence. I still wish he would trade in steaks and statin drugs for tofu and tabouli, but it looks like that isn't going to happen anytime soon. Our connections in other areas are profound, and living with and loving him over the years has given me a bounty of resources and ideas that have become the foundation and motivation for this book.

With great love,

Ellen

INTRODUCTION

When living with a partner who has fundamentally different values and life choices, it's important to determine your priorities and know your boundaries. This is especially critical if you're already in a long-term relationship and decide to go vegan and your partner doesn't.

Some vegans choose to break off a relationship when their diet becomes incompatible with their partner's. In many instances, though, there are compelling emotional, personal, and financial reasons to mend rather than end the relationship.

At my parents' fiftieth wedding anniversary, I asked my mother, "Mom, how did you do it? What's your secret to fifty years of wedded bliss?"

"One word," she quipped, without missing a beat, "tolerance."

"Tolerance of what?" I sassed back, as only the youngest child would.

"Don't go there" was all she said, with a wink.

I'm quite sure that if more of us believed in practicing tolerance, the divorce rate would be significantly lower. If you live with or have a relationship with someone who's happy-go-lucky and accepts whatever you do with a grain of salt, consider yourself fortunate indeed.

Although my motto is "It's more important to have someone who loves and respects me than to have a clone at the dinner table," it would be so much more convenient to have the clone. But the reality is, when you entered into your relationship, it's unlikely that specific meal plans were part of your long-term commitment. You probably couldn't have guessed that, at some point in the future, incompatibility in diet or lifestyle would become an issue.

As difficult as it may seem, the secret to living in harmony is accepting others just as they are. Focus on the person you *can* change: yourself. While it may be tempting to try to persuade others of the righteousness of your ways, that rarely

results in the desired outcome, and more often than not it leads to battles. As I've often told my children, sometimes it takes more strength and courage to walk away from a fight than to get into one.

Remember that it can take decades to become an "overnight success." People frequently ask me, "Doesn't everyone in your family eat the way you do when they see how healthy you are?" Although you might think my family would be lining up at the dinner table for the chance to eat like I do, they choose to stick with habits that are comfortable for them, regardless of how detrimental those habits may be to their health.

Change can feel threatening, especially when people are asked to consider options contrary to their long-held beliefs and penchants. Even when those options are highly beneficial, change is still often difficult. It can be particularly painful to admit to spouses or partners that they're right and make a good point. It can feel like caving in, swallowing one's pride, or losing one's identity or individuality. Although none of that is true, ego and emotions can occasionally get in the way of what's in a person's best interests. Sometimes it just seems easier to shut down rather than open up and try new ideas.

Developing acceptance is the task I've set before you. Instead of asking your partner to change, see how you can bridge your differences and make life in the kitchen easier, calmer, and more pleasant for both of you. Incredible things can happen when joyfulness, tolerance, and great food join forces.

chapter one

THE PRACTICAL SIDE OF A KITCHEN DIVIDED

One of the most effective ways of bringing many meat eaters around to an appreciation of vegan cuisine is to cook delicious vegan meals for them. This approach is often far more effective than any amount of preaching, and in these pages you'll find plenty of recipes that can help you implement this strategy. Still, at some point you'll need to sit down and hash out a joint approach to cooking and eating in your home. To that end, this chapter provides pointers on different systems you might implement and how to arrive at a solution that works for everyone.

CHOOSE AN APPROACH

There are many paths to achieving a peaceful and productive kitchen in a mixed-eating household. Here are the most workable approaches, along with guidelines on how to implement each. Choose the plan (or blend of plans) that best meets your needs and the needs of others in your household.

Peaceful Coexistence

- Each person does his or her own shopping, prep, cooking, and cleanup.
- Vegan and animal-based foods are stored on separate shelves in the pantry and refrigerator.

BENEFITS: This approach minimizes hassles and avoids arguments.

DRAWBACKS: Meal preparation and shopping aren't shared, and opportunities to connect and bond are lost. The vegan partner must make concessions in terms of seeing and smelling animal products.

1

Partial Coexistence

- One person buys all the food.
- Each person does his or her own cooking and cleanup.
- Vegan and animal-based foods are stored on separate shelves in the pantry and refrigerator.

BENEFITS: Shopping is simplified. If the nonvegan partner does the shopping, it can be an opportunity to learn more about plant-based foods.

DRAWBACKS: If the vegan partner does the shopping, values are compromised when purchasing animal products. The vegan partner must make concessions in terms of seeing and smelling animal products.

Conventional Roles

- One person does all the shopping, prep, cooking, and cleanup.

BENEFITS: This strategy minimizes hassles and avoids arguments.

DRAWBACKS: This approach can generate ongoing resentment. If the vegan partner does the shopping and cooking, values are compromised when purchasing and preparing animal products. The vegan partner must make concessions in terms of seeing and smelling animal products.

TIPS FROM THE TRENCHES

"My partner works in a steak house and isn't vegetarian, but he's extremely supportive. We make vegan meals that are easy to add meat to. Finding recipes that are flexible this way has been a huge help. Occasionally, we make separate dishes. No matter what, we always make sure it's a win-win!"

Division of Labor

- Everyone in the household is responsible for specific assigned tasks: shopping, prep, cooking, or cleanup. Responsibilities for each task are clearly defined.
- Constraints are delineated. For example, everyone adheres to rules about where meat and other animal products are stored in the refrigerator and which tools and equipment are acceptable to use for nonvegan prep and cooking.

BENEFITS: Efforts are equally distributed, everyone participates, and everyone has specific duties. Boundaries are set, and each person feels respected.

DRAWBACKS: Depending on how tasks are assigned, the vegan partner's values may be compromised when purchasing or preparing animal products or cleaning up after they're cooked. The vegan partner must make concessions in terms of seeing and smelling animal products.

Compromise

- Only vegan food is prepared and served in the house.
- The nonvegan partner can't bring animal-based food into the house but can eat it when dining out.

BENEFITS: This approach eliminates conflicts and provides opportunities for the nonvegan partner to try new foods and expand his or her culinary horizons.

DRAWBACKS: The nonvegan partner must make concessions at home and may feel resentful.

"Respect is the key. That's what makes any 'mixed marriage' work."

Middle Ground

- Primarily vegan food is prepared and served in the house, but the nonvegan partner may add animal products to plant-based dishes.
- The vegan partner does the shopping, prep, cooking, and cleanup for plant-based meals.
- The nonvegan partner does the shopping, prep, cooking, and cleanup for any animal products he or she chooses to add to the plant-based meals.
- Boundaries are set and strictly adhered to regarding where animal-based foods are stored in the refrigerator and which tools and equipment are acceptable to use for nonvegan food prep and cooking.

BENEFITS: This approach eliminates conflicts, engenders respect, and promotes tolerance. It also provides opportunities for the nonvegan partner to try new foods and expand his or her culinary horizons.

DRAWBACKS: The vegan partner must make concessions in terms of seeing and smelling animal products.

SET PRIORITIES

Regardless of individual eating styles, partners and other household members can make a list of their priorities to identify which values regarding diet and food are most important, which they're more flexible about, and which can be set aside. You can do this as a written exercise or just by talking.

First identify the positive attributes in your relationship and the values and beliefs you share. Realize that the foundation you've built is strong, and proceed in an atmosphere of trust, care, and concern for the relationship. Be honest but tactful. Give everyone space to share his or her feelings and beliefs without judgment. For example, if someone in the household is sickened by seeing or smelling fried chicken, acknowledge those feelings and consider making your home off limits to fried chicken out of respect for that person.

Communication about individual needs and how they can be honored will ultimately determine the success or failure of a divided kitchen. Jointly map out the future by identifying each person's constraints, establishing boundaries, and deciding what is truly important for the survival of your relationship and for everyone to thrive individually. Determine areas of potential compromise and trade-offs. For example, perhaps the nonvegan partner would be willing to forgo eating meat at home if the vegan partner would do most or all of the cooking. Alternatively, perhaps the vegan partner would tolerate cooked or prepared animal products being brought into the home if the nonvegan partner would commit to doing certain chores, such as car maintenance, laundry, or housecleaning.

ESTABLISH HELPFUL KITCHEN RITUALS AND ROUTINES

Here are some additional time-tested tips that may further promote peace in your kitchen:

- Stagger meal prep when you and your partner are making separate meals.
- Cook your meal in advance and heat it up at dinnertime. This will help minimize stress and save time when you have to prepare and cook a different meal for others later.
- Designate parts of the kitchen as vegan and nonvegan to avoid run-ins and prevent cross-contamination of foodstuffs.
- Assign an outdoor grill for the nonvegan partner to cook meat and other animal products on.

- Buy vegan meat alternatives. In addition to being convenient, mock meats are helpful transition foods for people who want to cut back on animal products. They can also be used as replacements for meat in conventional dishes.
- Make a game of cooking. Play music, dance, and laugh while you jointly prepare meals.
- Plan menus together.
- Plant a garden. Gardening is fun, practical, and economical. There's nothing quite as romantic or bonding as sharing a meal based on produce you jointly grew, harvested, and prepared.

USING THE RECIPES

The recipes in this book are designed to fit into menu plans for a divided kitchen in a variety of different ways. Use them however they will best suit you and your kitchen partner.

Satisfying Dishes with Meat and Dairy Alternatives

Some of the recipes in this book are prepared with protein-rich vegan meat alternatives (such as veggie burgers, vegan sausages, and seitan) and dairy products (such as vegan cheese). While whole, unprocessed plant foods offer the most nutritional bang for your buck, these tasty substitutes are great for providing the familiar flavors and textures meat eaters are accustomed to. The recipes that use these products are perfect for people who say things like "I'd sooner die than give up my steak." Here are a few go-to recipes in this category:

- Southwestern Fusion Stew (page 42)
- Bouillabaisse (page 43)
- Chili sin Carne (page 81)
- Quinoa Paella (page 88)
- Zucchini Boats with Kale and White Bean Filling (page 89)
- Fast 'n' Fabulous Cabbage (page 91)
- Quiche Your Troubles Good-Bye (page 92)
- No-Beef Bourguignon (page 98)
- Colorful Kabobs (page 99)
- Garlicky White Beans and Veggie Dogs (page 127)

Hearty Dishes Even a Meat Eater Will Love

You'll find many recipes for delicious, filling dishes made entirely with whole, unprocessed plant foods. Most meat eaters won't miss the meat or even think of adding a vegan meat substitute to these hearty dishes. Here's a small selection of the many such dishes in this book:

- Curried Rice Soup (page 34)
- Creamy Spinach Soup (page 39)
- Kitchen Sync Soup (page 40)
- Spinach Salad with Tempeh and Creamy Tarragon Dressing (page 53)
- Stealth Egg Salad (page 57)
- Make-Nice Niçoise Salad (page 58)
- Tofu Pad Thai (page 77)
- Some-Like-It-Hot Curry (page 78)
- Mushrooms and Lentils in Phyllo (page 94)
- Cajun Rice (page 124)

Flex Dishes

These recipes can serve as the nourishing center of a meal and need no accoutrements. Nevertheless, meat eaters can add meat or other animal products to them if they prefer. (However, once they see how much money can be saved by forgoing the meat and how delicious these dishes are without adding a thing, they may reconsider.) Here are some recipes that are sure winners in any flexitarian home:

- You-Say-Tomato Soup (page 33)
- Sweet Pea Soup (page 36)
- Manhattan Chowder (page 37)
- Please 'Em All Salad Bar (page 51)
- Toss-It-Together Stir-Fry (page 76)
- Overstuffed Soft Tacos (page 80)
- Bursting Burritos (page 82)
- Flexible Fajitas (page 84)
- Pasta Primavera (page 86)
- Garden Pizza (page 87)

"How do I manage family gatherings? Xanax. (Just kidding.) Actually, I bring a couple of side dishes and two desserts. I'm the lone vegan at family events."

Versatile Side Dishes

In addition to the dishes in chapter 8, Agreeable Appetizers and Simpatico Sides, check out the recipes in the soup and salads chapters (chapters 4 and 5). The delicious recipes in all three chapters are mostly quite easy to prepare, and meat eaters can enjoy them just as they would any side dish. To enjoy these recipes as a main course, vegans can either eat larger servings or include some plant-based high-protein foods, such as beans, tofu, or seitan. If you decide to take this approach, here are a few recipes that will fill the bill:

- Good-as-Gold Soup (page 32)
- Mushroom Extravaganza Soup (page 38)
- Something-for-Everyone Salad (page 50)
- Lemony Quinoa Tabouli (page 55)
- Rice Salad Dijon (page 56)
- Herbed Eggplant Slices (page 114)
- Roasted Vegetables (page 115)
- Potato Pancakes (page 118)
- As-You-Like-It Risotto (page 123)
- Kasha and Bows (page 125)

chapter two

NOURISHING OPTIONS TO BRIDGE THE DIVIDE

Many people who resist a vegan (or even vegetarian) diet cite concerns about not getting enough protein. However, it has been clearly proven that a well-rounded vegan diet that incorporates a wide variety of foods is perfectly adequate. Further, it isn't necessary to consume complete proteins or assiduously combine different foods to provide complete protein in any given meal. All foods contain amino acids (the building blocks of protein), and as long as the diet contains a diversity of foods, the body can synthesize protein from these building blocks. Still, it never hurts to allay fears about protein deficiency. Here's a rundown of some of the most protein-rich plant foods, which you may wish to emphasize in shared meals.

BROCCOLI. A nutritional powerhouse in many regards, broccoli also has an impressive protein content, with 5 grams of protein per cup. If you don't have time to make a separate protein dish for yourself, steamed broccoli is a great go-to solution.

LEGUMES. Beans (including soybeans), lentils, peanuts, and peas are all legumes. In addition to being a good source of protein, they're rich in fiber, filling, and inexpensive, especially if you purchase dried beans rather than canned. Most varieties of starchy beans contain 12 to 15 grams of protein per cup, and lentils provide 18 grams of protein per cup. Fresh soybeans, known as edamame, are a real standout when it comes to protein, containing about 17 grams of protein per cup of shelled edamame. Fresh peas are also a good source of protein, with 6.5 grams of protein per cup.

cooking grains

1. Measure out the amount of dry grains needed. For every 2½ cups of cooked grains, use about 1 cup of grains. (Certain grains will yield slightly more than 2½ cups.)

2. Drain in a colander or, for small grains like quinoa, a fine-mesh strainer, then rinse thoroughly.

3. Transfer to a saucepan and add water. For each cup of dry grains prior to soaking, use 1½ cups of water. If you didn't soak the grains, use 2 cups of water for each cup of grains.

4. Bring to a boil over high heat. Decrease the heat to medium-low, cover, and cook until all the liquid is absorbed and the grain is tender, using the amount of time indicated below as a guideline for each type of cooked grain called for in this book:

   Brown rice (any type): 40 to 45 minutes

   Brown and wild rice blend: 45 to 50 minutes

   Millet: 30 to 35 minutes

   Quinoa: 12 to 15 minutes

5. Turn off the heat and let stand, covered, for 5 minutes. Fluff with a fork.

MEAT ANALOGS. Vegan meat analogs (discussed later in this chapter) are typically a great source of protein. Many of them use high-protein soy or seitan as the base ingredient.

MILLET. Millet is a sweet, nutty-tasting whole grain that can be used in a variety of dishes from pilafs to stuffings to desserts. It's rich in protein, B vitamins, minerals, and the amino acid lysine. Plus, it is gluten-free.

NUTS AND SEEDS. Nuts and seeds, especially almonds, chia seeds, and sesame seeds, are high in calcium and protein and low in carbohydrates. Just 1 ounce of almonds (less than ¼ cup) contains 6 grams of protein. Nuts and seeds can be eaten raw or roasted, or they can be ground into nut or seed butter. In addition to using nuts and seeds in baking and as snacks, you can add them to salads, stews, and smoothies.

OATS. You may be surprised to learn that oats contain about 12 percent protein, and that the quality of their protein is almost equivalent to that of soy. Given that they also contain a generous complement of soluble fiber, oats are clearly a superior choice when it comes to nutrition.

QUINOA. High in protein and iron, quinoa has a pleasant nutty flavor and crunchy texture that even the most avid carnivore will love. It cooks up more quickly than most types of rice and is a great base for steamed vegetables. It shines when cooked and served cold in salads like tabouli and provides a wonderful canvas for gravies and sauces. In fact, quinoa contains so much protein (more than any other whole grain) that it's often a component in plant-based protein powder supplements.

SEITAN. Seitan, which is made from wheat gluten, has a texture amazingly similar to that of meat. Depending on how it's prepared, seitan can pass for meat in many dishes, making it an essential in a divided kitchen, as long as gluten or wheat intolerance isn't an issue. Seitan is the most densely packed source of vegetable protein known, with 20 to 30 grams of protein in a 4-ounce portion.

SOY MILK. Most forms of soy are very healthful, being loaded with phytochemicals thought to help reduce the risk of heart disease, osteoporosis, and cancer. While other forms of soy (such as tofu and tempeh) contain more protein per cup, you can't beat soy milk as a convenient way to boost the protein content of any meal. Pour it over cereal, blend it into a smoothie, mix unsweetened varieties into soups and sauces, or just drink it straight. However you use it, you'll be getting about 7 grams of protein per cup of soy milk.

SPINACH. On par with broccoli when it comes to protein, cooked spinach contains 5 grams of protein per cup. If you're short on time and need to add protein to a meal, a side of steamed spinach will do the trick nicely.

TEMPEH. Widely used in Thailand and Indonesia, tempeh is available in most well-stocked grocery stores in the United States. Made from fermented soybeans, it has a nutty flavor and a pleasantly chewy texture that makes it superior to tofu as a stand-in for meat.

TIPS FROM THE TRENCHES

"I eat what I eat, and she eats what she eats. We don't judge each other."

TOFU. Tofu has been a staple in Asia for about two thousand years. Known for its nutritional benefits and healthful phytochemicals, it's a versatile food that readily absorbs flavors from other ingredients, making it a good backdrop for familiar sauces. When crumbled, it's an excellent replacement for eggs in scrambled egg or quiche recipes. Plain tofu is widely available and comes in two main forms: regular (packed in water and refrigerated) and silken (in aseptic cartons and refrigerated tubs). Each type is available in soft, firm, and extra-firm varieties.

MEAT AND DAIRY ALTERNATIVES

The ever-increasing diversity of commercial vegan meat and dairy analogs is amazing. Gone are the days when just a few brands of veggie burgers and soy milk were available. Now you can purchase endless varieties of nondairy cheese, ice cream, milk, and yogurt, not to mention vegan beef, chicken, ham, turkey, and even seafood. Faux meats run the gamut from deli slices, sausages, and bacon to chicken tenders, nuggets, and wings, and some have such authentic flavor and texture that longtime vegetarians may find them unappealing. They tend to be highly processed, so if you're committed to mostly eating whole natural foods, you wouldn't want to make them a staple. However, they can make a huge difference in whether meat eaters find vegan dishes satisfying and can play an important role in transitioning to a plant-based diet.

CHEESE, VEGAN. The plethora of nondairy cheeses now available ranges from mozzarella and Cheddar to ricotta and cream cheese to Havarti and even American cheese (just in case you need an ersatz version of a food that was already ersatz to begin with). Base ingredients include almonds, rice, soy, and tapioca or arrowroot flour. I generally recommend those based on tapioca or arrowroot flour because they melt well.

ICE CREAM, VEGAN. For many people, ice cream is the ultimate in comfort food, yet it's packed with cholesterol and fat. While nondairy alternatives are also typically rich and can't exactly be called healthful, they are a better choice. They are typically made from almonds, coconut, hemp, rice, or soy and are offered in many flavors, so you're bound to find something to please the palates of nonvegans.

MEAT, VEGAN. With the many varieties of faux meat now available, from beef tips to hot dogs to chicken patties, you're sure to find several alternatives that your partner or other family members will enjoy. Try a variety of products to identify those your family prefers, then keep them on hand to add to vegan dishes to

vegan parmesan cheese

If you can't find vegan Parmesan cheese or just want to make your own, it's easy to put together. Simply combine ½ cup each of walnuts, sunflower seeds, and nutritional yeast with a pinch each of turmeric and salt in a food processor. Pulse until the nuts are finely ground. Makes about 1 cup. Stored in a container in the refrigerator, it will keep for 3 weeks.

make them heartier and more appealing to the meat eaters in your household. You'll find these vegan meats in supermarkets and natural food stores alongside other alternative products both in the frozen section and in the cold case.

MILK, NONDAIRY. Alternative milks are taking over shelves even at big-box stores. They've reached record sales as allergies to cow's milk soar and increasing numbers of people recognize the many benefits of a dairy-free diet. It used to be that the only alternative was soy milk, but the choices these days include versions made from almonds, coconut, hazelnuts, hemp, oats, rice, and sunflower seeds. Many are available in unsweetened, plain, vanilla, and sometimes other flavors, so there's bound to be a version that everyone in the household will enjoy.

TIPS FROM THE TRENCHES

"We can't force anyone to adopt our way of thinking. Love is about more than just liking the things in another person that reflect ourselves."

SEAFOOD, VEGAN. Vegan fish sticks and the like have been available for quite a while, but now you can purchase vegan prawns, shrimp, and even calamari, opening the door to vegan versions of classic seafood dishes. Vegan seafood may be stocked either in the cold case or in the frozen section of natural food stores and some grocery stores, alongside other alternative products.

SOUR CREAM, VEGAN. With all the rich flavor of conventional sour cream but none of the cholesterol, vegan sour cream is a win-win substitution in any kitchen, divided or not. If you'd like to make your own vegan sour cream at home, it's easy to do, and you can find plenty of recipes for it on the Internet or in other vegan cookbooks.

YOGURT, NONDAIRY. As with nondairy milks, the variety of nondairy yogurts available today is astounding. Base ingredients include almonds, coconut, rice, and soy. Numerous flavors are available, and you can now purchase even Greek-style nondairy yogurt. All of these alternatives contain living cultures, and most are good sources of calcium and protein. Although they're a bit spendy, they are generally highly acceptable to those who love dairy yogurts.

OTHER USEFUL INGREDIENTS

The recipes in this book primarily use familiar ingredients—mostly fresh vegetables and fruits, legumes, and whole grains. However, some of the ingredients called for are unusual, and in a few cases I have specific recommendations on products that are more healthful or will yield better results. Here's the scoop on those ingredients.

BALSAMIC VINEGAR. Hailing from Italy, where it's been produced for centuries, balsamic vinegar is made from white grapes and is aged for many years. For dark balsamic vinegar, the grapes are boiled for several hours to yield a sweet, almost syrupy vinegar. For white balsamic vinegar, the grapes are cooked at lower temperatures and yield a vinegar with a cleaner flavor and lighter color. I highly recommend seeking out fig-infused and pear-infused versions, which have even more complex flavors.

COCONUT MILK. Coconut milk is milk made from the meat of the coconut. Because it has a high fat content, I recommend using the light variety. Don't confuse it with coconut water, which is the liquid inside the coconut, or nondairy milks made from coconut.

EDAMAME. Edamame is a Japanese term for young green soybeans. Edamame is sold fresh at Asian markets and some specialty stores. It is available either shelled or unshelled in the refrigerated or frozen food section of most supermarkets and natural food stores. Like any legume, edamame must be cooked before being eaten, although fresh edamame could be considered a fast food, as it cooks in as little as five minutes.

ENER-G EGG REPLACER. Various brands of powdered egg replacers are available, but each uses a different amount of the powder and water to equal one egg. These recipes call for Ener-G egg replacer, which is available at natural food stores, in the natural food section of your supermarket, or online. With this brand, 1½ teaspoons of the powder plus 2 tablespoons of water equals one egg; this information may be helpful if you want to use a different egg replacer.

HOISIN SAUCE. With its complex salty-sweet flavor, hoisin sauce, a Chinese dipping sauce made from soybeans, vinegar, garlic, and chiles, is a quick and easy way to boost the flavor of savory dishes. Look for it at Asian markets or in the international foods section of mainstream grocery stores.

MISO. A salty, fermented paste that originated in Japan, miso is typically made from soybeans but may also contain other beans, grains, or a combination of beans and grains. Because there are many varieties, miso can range in color from light to dark and in taste from mild to robust. Lighter versions tend to be milder and less salty, and darker kinds tend to have a more full-bodied flavor. When adding miso to soup, do so after the soup has been removed from the heat. That will protect the active enzymes and probiotics in the miso.

SOY SAUCE. In any recipe that calls for soy sauce, feel free to substitute tamari, shoyu, or Bragg Liquid Aminos. As soy sauce is very high in sodium, use low- or reduced-sodium varieties if available.

TORTILLAS. For optimum flavor and nutrition, choose tortillas made from sprouted corn or sprouted whole grains. Several gluten-free varieties are available, made with brown rice, millet, and teff, among other ingredients.

TIPS FROM THE TRENCHES

"I'm a new vegan, and as a stay-at-home mom, I don't feel comfortable asking my husband to make his own meals. I usually end up making two different dishes or one that I can add meat to. But it's hard for me to touch meat anymore; it's becoming unappetizing. Still, I think that it's important to respect the right of other adults to make their own choices. Finding balance is my goal. My husband is open to vegetarian meals, so at least I have some wiggle room."

VEGETABLE BROTH POWDER. Many of my recipes call for vegetable broth powder, which is economical, flavorful, and convenient; it's also easy to store and has a long shelf life. I recommend Vogue Cuisine Instant VegeBase. It's the lowest in sodium, is gluten-free, and adds complex flavor, not just saltiness, as most broth powders do.

chapter three

NEW BEGINNINGS BREAKFASTS

Even if you get up on the right side of the bed, you can't start off on the right foot if your day begins with arguments about food. Yet mornings can be busy and all too stressful as everyone scrambles to get out the door on time. The recipes in this chapter will help you provide delicious vegan options with a minimum of muss and fuss. Some of them are highly portable and can be prepared in advance, so now there's no excuse for anyone to skip the most important meal of the day.

Pluots, a hybrid of plums and apricots, often have deep purple flesh, making them as attractive as they are juicy and flavorful. They give this smoothie wonderful eye appeal!

soothing SMOOTHIES

2 frozen **bananas,** broken into chunks

2 cups **nondairy milk**

1 cup frozen or fresh **blueberries**

3 **pluots,** pitted

8 frozen **peach slices,** or 1 large fresh peach, sliced

Ice cubes, if needed

Put all the ingredients in a blender and process until smooth. If using fresh blueberries or peach, you may want to add a few ice cubes to chill the smoothie and achieve the desired consistency.

Per serving: 277 calories, 4 g protein, 4 g fat (0.4 g sat), 60 g carbs, 183 mg sodium, 465 mg calcium, 9 g fiber

Note: Analyzed with unsweetened almond milk.

If you can't physically change your latitude, maybe a dessert from the tropics can provide a welcome attitude adjustment.

CHANGES-IN-ATTITUDE smoothies

2 frozen **bananas,** broken into chunks

1 **mango,** cut into large pieces (see tip, page 47), or 8 ounces frozen mango chunks

½ **papaya,** cut into large pieces (optional)

1 cup **ice cubes**

4 fresh or canned **pineapple rings,** or 12 frozen or fresh **strawberries**

4 pitted **soft dates,** preferably medjool

3 tablespoons unsweetened shredded dried **coconut**

Put all the ingredients in a blender and process until smooth.

Per serving: 441 calories, 4 g protein, 6 g fat (5 g sat), 104 g carbs, 8 mg sodium, 69 mg calcium, 12 g fiber

TROPICAL FRUIT SALAD: This combination also makes a great fruit salad. Simply forgo the ice and use all fresh fruits rather than frozen. Cut the fruits into bite-sized pieces, put them in a bowl, and stir gently to combine. Serve topped with the coconut.

TIPS FROM THE TRENCHES

"I'm lucky to have a very supportive and open-minded partner. I never try to convert her, and she's slowly making her own changes, which is interesting and obviously very welcome."

Including oats in smoothies may seem unusual, but trust me: in addition to being highly nutritious, this breakfast shake is delicious. Plus, the oats provide more sustained energy than typical smoothie ingredients. Best of all, this breakfast treat is like a portable bowl of oatmeal, allowing you and yours to meet your nutritional needs even on busy mornings.

OATY on-the-go SMOOTHIES

MAKES 2 SERVINGS

2 small **bananas**

2 small **apples,** cored and quartered

1 cup vanilla **nondairy yogurt**

1/3 cup old-fashioned **rolled oats**

3/4 teaspoon ground **cinnamon**

Water, as desired

1/4 cup **raisins**

Put the bananas, apples, yogurt, oats, and cinnamon in a blender and process until creamy. For a thinner consistency, add up to 1 cup of water and blend again. Add the raisins and pulse until they are combined but not completely broken down.

Per serving: 377 calories, 8 g protein, 4 g fat (1 g sat), 83 g carbs, 47 mg sodium, 147 mg calcium, 11 g fiber

Note: Analyzed with vanilla soy yogurt.

TIP: Personally, I like a bit of texture from the oats in my smoothie, but if you prefer a smoother consistency, put the oats in the blender first and process them briefly before adding the remaining ingredients.

Cheddar Drop Biscuits, *page 27*

Nothing-Fishy Ceviche, *page 31*

Mornings can be so hectic. To put some satisfying crunch into crunch time, whip up this smoothie and you'll be good to go—or better. The nuts provide plenty of protein and healthful fats, so this smoothie can tide you over for hours.

crunch-time SMOOTHIES

2 frozen **bananas,** broken into chunks

2 cups **nondairy milk**

2 tablespoons raw or unsalted roasted **almonds**

2 tablespoons raw or unsalted roasted **cashews**

2 tablespoons unsalted roasted **peanuts**

2 tablespoons unsalted **pistachio nuts**

Put all the ingredients in a blender and process until mostly smooth but some texture remains.

Per serving: 329 calories, 9 g protein, 14 g fat (2 g sat), 35 g carbs, 184 mg sodium, 501 mg calcium, 5 g fiber

Note: Analyzed with unsweetened almond milk.

TIPS FROM THE TRENCHES

"When my boyfriend expresses surprise at how delicious vegan food is—which he often does—I never say, 'I told you so!' Instead, I simply say, 'I'm so glad that you liked it!'"

It's always a good idea to sit down to eat. However, sometimes life doesn't cooperate. When that happens, this smoothie will save the day. It's rich in energy and healthful omega-3 fats from hemp and chia seeds, so it will keep you full and satisfied till lunchtime or beyond.

energy-rich GREEN SMOOTHIES

2 frozen **bananas,** broken into chunks

2 cups **nondairy milk**

2 leaves **kale,** stemmed and coarsely chopped, or 1 cup **baby spinach,** lightly packed

4 pitted **soft dates,** preferably medjool (optional)

3 tablespoons unsalted roasted **peanuts** or other nuts

3 tablespoons raw or unsalted roasted **sunflower seeds**

2 tablespoons **hemp** or **chia seeds**

Put all the ingredients in a blender and process until smooth.

Per serving: 481 calories, 13 g protein, 20 g fat (3 g sat), 72 g carbs, 197 mg sodium, 561 mg calcium, 10 g fiber

Note: Analyzed with unsweetened almond milk.

This spread, made with only fruit, nuts, and seeds, is packed with protein and healthful carbs. Try it on toast for a cheery wake-up call—and for sustained energy that will keep you going for hours. It's also a perfect recovery snack after a vigorous workout.

SUNSHINE ALMOND-MANGO **spread**

MAKES 8 SERVINGS

3 **mangoes,** cut into large pieces (see tip, page 47), or 24 ounces frozen mango chunks, thawed

1½ cups chopped raw or unsalted roasted **almonds**

¾ cup pitted **soft dates,** preferably medjool

¾ cup **raisins**

⅓ cup raw **sunflower seeds**

Put all the ingredients in a food processor and process until smooth. Stored in a sealed container in the refrigerator, the spread will keep for 1 week.

Per serving: 335 calories, 7 g protein, 4 g fat (1 g sat), 49 g carbs, 4 mg sodium, 91 mg calcium, 5 g fiber

TIPS FROM THE TRENCHES

"I don't think it's a question of coping; it's about honoring and growing. When I first became vegan, I designated two shelves in the pantry and two crispers in the refrigerator for nonvegan food. This meant that my husband could eat everything in the house, and I could eat everything not on those shelves or in those crispers. It's been a perfect solution for us."

This high-fiber breakfast treat provides a powerful energy boost thanks to the dates, while the nuts will sustain you for hours. The squares must be refrigerated for at least two hours to firm up, so you may want to make them the night before.

DATE AND NUT **squares**

2 cups unsalted roasted **almonds**

½ cup unsalted roasted **peanuts**

4 cups pitted **soft dates,** preferably medjool

2 tablespoons unsweetened chunky **peanut butter** or other nut butter

Put the almonds and peanuts in a food processor and pulse until finely chopped. Don't overprocess, or you'll end up with nut butter. Transfer to a medium bowl.

Put the dates in the food processor and pulse until finely chopped. Add the peanut butter and pulse until well combined. Add the almonds and peanuts and pulse until evenly incorporated.

Line an 8-inch square baking pan with parchment paper. Transfer the mixture to the lined pan and press it in an even layer, smoothing the top. Cover and refrigerate for at least 2 hours, until firm. Cut into 9 squares. Because the squares will be a bit sticky, you may want to individually wrap them in waxed paper or plastic wrap.

Per serving: 417 calories, 10 g protein, 17 g fat (2 g sat), 64 g carbs, 19 mg sodium, 112 mg calcium, 9 g fiber

DATE AND NUT BALLS: Line a small baking sheet with parchment paper. Using moistened hands, form the mixture into 9 balls. Put the balls on the lined baking sheet and refrigerate for at least 2 hours, until firm.

Muesli may just be the ultimate in easy, versatile breakfast food. Once it's mixed together, your options for serving it are almost unlimited. Whether eating it hot or cold, you can take it over the top by adding fresh or dried fruit, such as berries, chopped apples, sliced bananas, currants, dates, or raisins.

seeded MUESLI

2 cups old-fashioned **rolled oats**

1 cup **rye flakes** or additional rolled oats

1/2 cup raw or unsalted roasted **sunflower seeds**

1/2 cup **sesame seeds**

1/4 cup sliced **almonds**

1/4 cup coarsely chopped **walnuts**

1/4 cup **oat bran or wheat bran**

1/4 cup raw or toasted **wheat germ**

Put all the ingredients in a large bowl and stir to combine. Stored in a sealed container at room temperature, the muesli will keep for 2 months.

Per 1/2 cup: 231 calories, 9 g protein, 11 g fat (1 g sat), 26 g carbs, 1 mg sodium, 11 mg calcium, 5 g fiber

TIPS

- For a porridge, cook the muesli up in a one-to-one ratio with nondairy milk or water.
- For a cold cereal, soak it in cold water, fruit juice, or nondairy milk or yogurt to soften the grains, using about two parts liquid to one part muesli.
- You can customize the basic muesli mix to suit your taste, substituting different nuts, seeds, or flaked grains as you wish.

It's so easy to get along when the smell of warm pancakes fills the air. Plus, the batter for these pancakes can be prepared in a food processor, streamlining the process and making it easier to share the kitchen if others are preparing something else for breakfast.

FAST-TRACK SEEDED **blueberry** PANCAKES

MAKES 12 PANCAKES, 4 SERVINGS

1½ cups plain or vanilla **nondairy milk**

¾ cup whole wheat **flour**

1 teaspoon **baking powder**

¼ teaspoon **baking soda**

¼ teaspoon ground **cinnamon**

¼ teaspoon **salt** (optional)

1 cup old-fashioned **rolled oats**

¼ cup raw **sunflower seeds**

2 tablespoons chopped **walnuts**

½ cup fresh **blueberries**

Put the nondairy milk, flour, baking powder, baking soda, cinnamon, and optional salt in a food processor and process until well combined. Add the oats through the chute and pulse until they are combined but not completely broken down. Add the sunflower seeds and walnuts through the chute and pulse until combined. Let the batter rest for 5 to 10 minutes.

Preheat the oven to 300 degrees F. Have a nonstick baking sheet ready or line a baking sheet with parchment paper.

Heat a large nonstick skillet over medium-high heat until a drop of water sizzles and dances on the surface. With a ladle or large spoon, portion the batter onto the skillet using about ¼ cup per pancake. Give the pancakes plenty of room in the skillet so they can spread (they should be thin, only about ¼ inch thick). When the skillet is full, place several blueberries on the surface of each pancake.

Decrease the heat to medium-low and cook until bubbles appear on the tops of the pancakes and the bottoms are golden brown, about 4 minutes. Gently flip the pancakes and cook until golden brown on the other side, about 4 minutes longer. Transfer the pancakes to the baking sheet and put them in the oven to keep warm while you cook the remaining pancakes.

Per serving (3 pancakes): 251 calories, 9 g protein, 10 g fat (1 g sat), 36 g carbs, 221 mg sodium, 277 mg calcium, 5 g fiber

Note: Analyzed with unsweetened almond milk.

These vegan biscuits are savory, portable, and highly addictive! The nondairy yogurt creates a tender crumb and complements the tangy vegan cheese.

CHEDDAR DROP **biscuits**

See photo facing page 20.

MAKES 12 BISCUITS

2 cups whole wheat **flour**

1 tablespoon **baking powder**

½ teaspoon **baking soda**

½ teaspoon **salt**

¼ cup nonhydrogenated vegan **margarine** or shortening

¾ cup shredded vegan **Cheddar cheese**

1 tablespoon finely chopped **onion** (optional)

1 tablespoon finely chopped green or red **bell pepper** (optional)

1½ cups plain vegan **yogurt**

Preheat the oven to 425 degrees F. Line a baking sheet with parchment paper or mist it with cooking spray.

Put the flour, baking powder, baking soda, and salt into a food processor and pulse eight times to combine. Cut the vegan margarine into eight pieces, drop the pieces into the flour mixture, and pulse eight times. Add the vegan cheese and optional vegetables and pulse four times.

Transfer to a medium bowl. Add the vegan yogurt and stir just until combined. For each biscuit, drop ¼ cup of the dough onto the lined baking sheet.

Bake for 15 to 20 minutes, until firm and golden brown.

Per biscuit: 146 calories, 4 g protein, 6 g fat (2 g sat), 20 g carbs, 318 mg sodium, 110 mg calcium, 2 g fiber

Note: Analyzed with plain soy yogurt and Daiya Cheddar-style shreds.

TIP: Feel free to play with the vegetables in this recipe. You can add more vegetables or substitute other vegetables for the onion and bell pepper. Just keep the total amount of vegetables to about ¼ cup or less so the biscuits hold together well. Chopped mushrooms, green onions, black olives, tomatoes, roasted red bell peppers, and parsley are just a few of the possibilities.

chapter four

SOOTHING SOUPS

Soups are a great way to introduce others to a delectable variety of vegetables full of vibrant color and healthful nutrients. The simpler soups in this chapter can be served as the prelude to a meal, or you can use them as a base and add grains, beans, plant-based proteins, or a combination for a heartier soup to be served as a main course. If you're living with a kitchen divided, others can add whatever they like to the soup and you don't have to know about it. Or, in the best-case scenario, they'll realize that the vegan version is not only delicious and filling but also more economical. As a bonus, most soups store well in the refrigerator, where they'll be at the ready when you don't have much time to prepare a meal.

If the nonvegan in your household is male, as is often the case, you may not be able to convince him that a plant-based diet is manly. But perhaps you can up the ante and dare him to add more hot sauce to this gazpacho. That should put some hair on his chest! Alternatively, if you're in the position of cooking nonvegan food for others, this recipe will come to your rescue. Think of it as a salad in a glass.

macho GAZPACHO

MAKES 4 SERVINGS

1 **cucumber,** coarsely chopped

1 **green bell pepper,** quartered

1 large ripe **tomato,** quartered

1 **green onion,** trimmed

2 tablespoons chopped fresh **parsley**

1 clove **garlic,** coarsely chopped

8 cups low-sodium spicy **vegetable juice**

2 tablespoons red wine **vinegar**

1 tablespoon vegan **Worcestershire sauce** (optional)

$\frac{1}{8}$ teaspoon **hot sauce,** plus more if desired (optional)

Pinch ground **pepper**

Salt

1 ripe **avocado,** diced (optional)

Put the cucumber, bell pepper, tomato, green onion, parsley, garlic, and 3 cups of the vegetable juice in a blender. Process in short bursts until the vegetables are finely chopped but still have some texture. (Alternatively, finely chop the cucumber, bell pepper, tomato, green onion, parsley, and garlic by hand.)

Transfer to a glass or stainless steel container and stir in the remaining 5 cups of vegetable juice and the vinegar, optional vegan Worcestershire sauce, optional hot sauce, pepper, and salt to taste. Cover and refrigerate for at least 1 hour, until well chilled. Serve cold, topped with avocado if desired.

Per serving: 128 calories, 5 g protein, 0.2 g fat (0 g sat), 26 g carbs, 286 mg sodium, 59 mg calcium, 6 g fiber

TIP: Gazpacho is so easy to put together, and it can sit in the refrigerator for several days. It's also very portable, so it makes an easy-to-pack light lunch.

Great news! You can leave the fish in the ocean and still enjoy delicious ceviche, a classic tropical dish that conjures up images of dining oceanside along the Caribbean. This recipe calls for vegan prawns, which can be found at many Asian markets and have recently become more available in well-stocked supermarkets and natural food stores. Look for them with other meat substitutes in the freezer or cold case.

NOTHING-FISHY ceviche

See photo facing page 21.

MAKES 4 SERVINGS

1 package (8.8 ounces) **vegan prawns or shrimp,** thawed if frozen, cut into bite-sized pieces

2 ripe **tomatoes,** diced

1 cup freshly squeezed **lime juice**

½ small **red bell pepper,** chopped

¼ cup finely chopped **red onion**

1 stalk **celery,** finely chopped

1 tablespoon chopped fresh **cilantro**

1 tablespoon chopped fresh **parsley**

1 clove **garlic,** finely chopped

Salt

Ground **pepper**

1 ripe **avocado**

2 tablespoons freshly squeezed **lemon juice**

4 sprigs **parsley,** for garnish

4 slices **lime,** for garnish

Put the vegan prawns, tomatoes, lime juice, bell pepper, onion, celery, cilantro, parsley, and garlic in a medium stainless steel or glass bowl and stir to combine. Cover and refrigerate for at least 4 hours or up to 24 hours, stirring occasionally. Season with salt and pepper to taste.

Just before serving, cut the avocado in half, remove the pit, and cut the flesh into bite-sized pieces. Put the avocado in a small bowl, sprinkle with the lemon juice to prevent browning, and stir gently.

Portion the prawn mixture into individual bowls and top with the avocado. Garnish each serving with a parsley sprig and a lime slice.

Per serving: 159 calories, 3 g protein, 8 g fat (1 g sat), 25 g carbs, 135 mg sodium, 109 mg calcium, 7 g fiber

Note: Analysis doesn't include salt to taste or parsley and lime for garnish.

Beta-carotene and vitamin C are highlighted in this brightly colored soup. Between those nutrients and the intoxicating flavor, this soup may just help keep you and your beloved healthy and harmonious, making it as valuable as gold, if not more so.

GOOD-AS-GOLD soup

See photo facing page 52.

MAKES 4 SERVINGS

4 cups **water**

12 **carrots,** cut into 1-inch-thick rounds

2 **onions,** chopped

2 cloves **garlic,** chopped

1 **orange,** peeled, sectioned, seeded, and cut into pieces

4 tablespoons low-sodium **vegetable broth powder**

1 teaspoon grated fresh **ginger**

Salt

1 tablespoon chopped fresh **chives,** for garnish

Put ½ cup of the water in a large pot, then add the carrots, onions, and garlic. Cook over medium heat, stirring occasionally and adding more water as needed to prevent sticking, until the onions are translucent, about 10 minutes.

Stir in the remaining water and the orange and broth powder and bring to a boil over high heat. Decrease the heat to medium-low, cover, and cook, stirring occasionally, until the carrots are tender, about 10 minutes.

Stir in the ginger, cover, and cook for 5 minutes. Season with salt to taste. Serve hot or cold, garnished with the chives.

Per serving: 148 calories, 3 g protein, 1 g fat (0.1 g sat), 35 g carbs, 139 mg sodium, 103 mg calcium, 7 g fiber

Note: Analysis doesn't include salt to taste or chives for garnish.

TIPS FROM THE TRENCHES

"I haven't shoved my vegan ways down my husband's throat, and guess what? Now he's coming up with meatless alternatives himself!"

If Fred Astaire and Ginger Rogers had whipped up a batch of this soup instead of focusing on phonetics, perhaps their romance wouldn't have fallen flat in the film *Shall We Dance*. Fortunately, you need not follow in their fancy footsteps. Think of this soup as a basic bouillabaisse broth that diners can customize to suit their dietary preferences by adding faux seafood, beans, tofu, or whatever their hearts desire.

YOU-SAY-**tomato** SOUP

½ cup **water,** plus more as needed

1 large **leek** (white and tender green parts only), cut into ½-inch-thick rounds

1 cup chopped **yellow onion**

4 cloves **garlic,** chopped

4 cups no-salt-added **vegetable broth**

3 cups chopped fresh or no-salt-added canned **tomatoes** with liquid

1 can (15 ounces) no-salt-added **tomato sauce**

½ cup chopped fresh flat-leaf **parsley,** lightly packed

2 tablespoons chopped fresh **thyme,** or 2 teaspoons dried

1 **bay leaf**

2 teaspoons whole-grain **flour**

1½ teaspoons **saffron threads** (optional)

Salt

Flat-leaf **parsley** leaves, for garnish

Put the water in a large pot, then add the leek, onion, and garlic. Cook over medium heat, stirring occasionally and adding more water as needed to prevent sticking, until the leek and onion are tender, about 15 minutes.

Stir in the broth, tomatoes, tomato sauce, parsley, thyme, and bay leaf and bring to a boil over high heat. Decrease the heat to medium-low, cover, and cook until heated through, about 5 minutes.

Ladle about ½ cup of the broth into a small bowl. Stir in the flour, then stir the mixture into the soup. Stir in the optional saffron and cook for 5 minutes, stirring occasionally. Season with salt to taste. Serve hot or cold, garnished with parsley leaves.

Per serving: 142 calories, 5 g protein, 0.2 g fat (0 g sat), 29 g carbs, 54 mg sodium, 171 mg calcium, 7 g fiber

Note: Analysis doesn't include salt to taste or parsley for garnish.

The next time others voice their (erroneous) concerns about lack of protein in a vegan diet, don't argue. Instead, just set a bowl of this sophisticated, fragrant soup in front of them and let the alluring aroma do the work for you.

curried RICE SOUP

5 cups **water**

2 **yellow onions,** chopped

2 **carrots,** chopped

2 tablespoons **curry powder**

1 cup long-grain **brown rice** or brown and wild rice blend

5 tablespoons low-sodium **vegetable broth powder**

1 can (15 ounces) no-salt-added **Great Northern beans,** drained and rinsed

Salt

2 tablespoons chopped fresh **parsley,** for garnish

Put ½ cup of the water in a large pot, then add the onions, carrots, and curry powder. Cook over medium heat, stirring occasionally and adding more water as needed to prevent sticking, until the onions are translucent, about 10 minutes.

Stir in the remaining water and the rice and broth powder and bring to a boil over high heat. Decrease the heat to medium-low, cover, and cook, stirring occasionally, until the rice is tender, about 50 minutes.

Add the beans and cook, stirring occasionally, until they are heated through, about 5 minutes. Using a handheld blender, or using a standard blender and working in batches if need be, process the soup in short bursts to achieve the desired texture. Some texture should still remain. Season with salt to taste. Serve hot or cold, garnished with the parsley.

Per serving: 346 calories, 11 g protein, 3 g fat (0.4 g sat), 71 g carbs, 335 mg sodium, 100 mg calcium, 12 g fiber

Note: Analysis doesn't include salt to taste or parsley for garnish.

This is the ultimate replacement for chicken soup. Miso is my favorite soup base, hands down. Known for its beneficial probiotics and enzymes that promote healing and good digestion, miso is pleasantly but not-too-intensely salty. Hijiki and arame are sea vegetables; look for them in natural food stores and international markets.

MELLOW **miso** SOUP

MAKES 4 SERVINGS

6 cups **water**

2 ounces **hijiki or arame**

14 ounces **firm or extra-firm tofu,** cut into small cubes

2 cups shredded green or napa **cabbage**

Noodles from 2 packages (2.1 ounces each) **ramen**

8 ounces fresh **shiitake** or other mushrooms, sliced (optional)

2 **green onions,** thinly sliced

¼ cup white or red **miso**

Put 2 cups of the water in a medium bowl. Add the hijiki and let soak until tender, about 20 minutes.

Put the remaining 4 cups of water in a medium pot and bring to a boil over high heat. Decrease the heat to medium-high. Stir in the tofu, cabbage, and ramen noodles and return to a boil. Decrease the heat to medium-low and stir in the optional mushrooms and half of the green onion. Cook, stirring occasionally, until the ramen is tender and the noodles have separated, 3 to 5 minutes.

Drain the hijiki, then rinse and drain again. Stir the hijiki into the soup. Remove from the heat.

Ladle about 1 cup of the broth into a bowl. Add the miso and stir to combine, then stir the mixture into the soup. Serve immediately, garnished with the remaining green onion.

Per serving: 253 calories, 10 g protein, 8 g fat (3 g sat), 38 g carbs, 589 mg sodium, 267 mg calcium, 8 g fiber

This satisfying soup doesn't contain any "mystery" ingredients and will appeal to anyone, vegan or otherwise. And even if you and your partner aren't just like two peas in a pod after sharing this soup, at least you will have given peas a chance.

sweet PEA SOUP

6 cups **water**

1 **onion,** chopped

2 **carrots,** chopped

2 stalks **celery,** chopped

2 large **potatoes,** scrubbed and chopped

6 tablespoons low-sodium **vegetable broth powder**

2 small **zucchini,** chopped

2 ripe **tomatoes,** chopped

2 cups fresh or frozen **peas**

1 cup fresh or frozen **corn kernels**

1 clove **garlic,** finely chopped

1 teaspoon dried **basil**

1 teaspoon dried **parsley**

Salt

Put ½ cup of the water in a large pot, then add the onion, carrots, and celery. Cook over medium heat, stirring occasionally and adding more water as needed to prevent sticking, until the onion is translucent, about 10 minutes.

Stir in the remaining water and the potatoes and broth powder and bring to a boil over high heat. Decrease the heat to medium-low, cover, and cook, stirring occasionally, until the potatoes are tender, about 15 minutes.

Stir in the zucchini, tomatoes, peas, corn, garlic, basil, and parsley and cook, stirring occasionally, until the zucchini is tender, about 10 minutes. Season with salt to taste. Serve hot.

Per serving: 245 calories, 9 g protein, 0.4 g fat (0.1 g sat), 52 g carbs, 165 mg sodium, 71 mg calcium, 9 g fiber

Note: Analysis doesn't include salt to taste.

TIPS

- To beef up this soup and serve it as a main dish, add up to 3 cups of cooked whole grains, such as brown rice or millet (see page 11), when adding the zucchini.

- Because the ingredients in this recipe are so simple and relatively neutral tasting, the soup makes a good base for the addition of plant-based meat alternatives.

- For a richer-flavored broth, add 2 tablespoons of white or red miso after removing the soup from the heat. To ensure the miso is evenly incorporated, first mix it with about 1 cup of the broth.

Cozy and comforting, this red, Manhattan-style chowder will keep your home fires burning. To serve this soup as a main course, add vegan seafood, canned beans, or other plant-based proteins.

MANHATTAN chowder

5 cups **water**

2 cups chopped **yellow onions**

1 cup chopped **celery**

1 can (28 ounces) no-salt-added chopped **tomatoes**

2 **waxy potatoes,** such as red or Yukon gold, scrubbed and chopped

1 cup chopped fresh flat-leaf **parsley,** lightly packed

1½ teaspoons dried **thyme**

1 teaspoon dried **oregano**

1 **bay leaf**

Salt

Put ½ cup of the water in a large pot, then add the onions and celery. Cook over medium heat, stirring occasionally and adding more water as needed to prevent sticking, until the onions are translucent, about 10 minutes.

Stir in the remaining water and the tomatoes, potatoes, parsley, thyme, oregano, and bay leaf and bring to a boil over high heat. Decrease the heat to medium-low, cover, and cook, stirring occasionally, until the potatoes are tender, about 15 minutes. Remove the bay leaf and season with salt to taste. Serve hot.

Per serving: 151 calories, 4 g protein, 0.2 g fat (0.1 g sat), 33 g carbs, 42 mg sodium, 188 mg calcium, 5 g fiber

Note: Analysis doesn't include salt to taste.

Mushrooms are widely touted for their anticancer properties. They are also an excellent meat substitute, thanks to their texture and abundant flavor, not to mention the fact that they're cholesterol-free and much lower in fat and calories than meat is. The more varieties of mushrooms you can pack into this soup, the tastier it will be!

mushroom EXTRAVAGANZA SOUP

MAKES 4 SERVINGS

5 cups **water**

1 **yellow onion,** chopped

1 stalk **celery,** chopped

1¼ pounds mixed **mushrooms,** such as shiitake, portobello, porcini, oyster, and button, sliced

5 tablespoons low-sodium **vegetable broth powder**

¼ cup long-grain **brown rice**

2 tablespoons reduced-sodium **soy sauce**

1 cup unsweetened nondairy milk or light **coconut milk** (optional)

Salt

Ground **pepper**

Chopped fresh **parsley,** for garnish

Sliced **almonds,** for garnish

Put ½ cup of the water in a large pot, then add the onion and celery. Cook over medium heat, stirring occasionally and adding more water as needed to prevent sticking, until the onion is translucent, about 10 minutes.

Stir in the remaining water and the mushrooms, broth powder, rice, and soy sauce and bring to a boil over high heat. Decrease the heat to medium-low, cover, and cook, stirring occasionally until the rice is tender, about 45 minutes.

Stir in the optional nondairy milk and season with salt and pepper to taste. If you wish, use an immersion blender to create a smoother texture. Serve hot, garnished with parsley and almonds.

Per serving: 121 calories, 6 g protein, 1 g fat (0.1 g sat), 24 g carbs, 27 mg sodium, 26 mg calcium, 3 g fiber

Note: Analysis doesn't include salt to taste or parsley and almonds for garnish.

Between the spinach, peas, and cannellini beans, this substantial soup is a protein powerhouse!

creamy SPINACH SOUP

3 cups **water**

2 cups chopped **yellow onions**

4 cloves **garlic,** chopped

2 cans (15 ounces each) no-salt-added **cannellini beans,** drained, rinsed, and lightly mashed

1 pound fresh **spinach,** coarsely chopped, or 1 package (10 ounces) frozen chopped spinach

10 ounces frozen **peas**

3 tablespoons low-sodium **vegetable broth powder**

Salt

Ground **pepper**

Put ½ cup of the water in a large pot, then add the onions and garlic. Cook over medium heat, stirring occasionally and adding more water as needed to prevent sticking, until the onions are tender, about 15 minutes.

Stir in the remaining water and the beans, spinach, peas, and broth powder and bring to a boil over high heat. Decrease the heat to medium-low, cover, and cook, stirring occasionally, until all the vegetables are tender, about 10 minutes. Season with salt and pepper to taste. If you wish, use an immersion blender to create a smoother texture. Serve hot.

Per serving: 313 calories, 16 g protein, 1.8 g fat (0 g sat), 58 g carbs, 221 mg sodium, 195 mg calcium, 18 g fiber

Note: Analysis doesn't include salt to taste.

RICH-AND-CREAMY SPINACH SOUP: Substitute 1 can (15 ounces) of light coconut milk for 2 cups of the water.

CHUNKY SPINACH-POTATO SOUP: Add 2 potatoes, scrubbed and chopped, when adding the beans. Cook until the potatoes are tender, about 20 minutes, before seasoning with salt and pepper and serving.

At first glance, this fabulous chunky soup may seem to contain everything but the kitchen sink. Thanks to the beans and mushrooms, it offers so much flavor, texture, and nutrition that it will satisfy even the most die-hard meat eater.

kitchen SYNC SOUP

4 cups **water**

1 **onion,** chopped

2 **carrots,** cut into $\frac{1}{2}$-inch-thick rounds

4 ounces **mushrooms,** sliced

2 stalks **celery,** chopped

2 cloves **garlic,** chopped

2 cups chopped **broccoli**

1 **potato,** scrubbed and chopped

1 small **zucchini,** chopped

1 small **yellow summer squash,** chopped

1 cup cut fresh or frozen **green beans**

Put $\frac{1}{2}$ cup of the water in a large pot, then add the onion, carrots, mushrooms, celery, and garlic. Cook over medium heat, stirring occasionally and adding more water as needed to prevent sticking, until the onion is translucent, about 10 minutes.

Stir in the remaining water and the broccoli, potato, zucchini, yellow squash, and green beans and bring to a boil over high heat. Decrease the heat to medium-low, cover, and cook, stirring occasionally, until the potatoes are tender, about 15 minutes.

1 can (28 ounces) no-salt-added chopped **tomatoes**

2 cups stemmed and chopped **spinach or collard greens,** lightly packed

1 can (15 ounces) no-salt-added **kidney beans,** drained and rinsed

1 can (15 ounces) no-salt-added **garbanzo beans,** drained and rinsed

2 tablespoons chopped fresh **parsley**

2 tablespoons **Italian seasoning**

Salt

Parsley sprigs, for garnish

Stir in the tomatoes, spinach, kidney beans, garbanzo beans, parsley, and Italian seasoning. Cook, stirring occasionally, until all the vegetables are tender, about 10 minutes. Season with salt to taste. Serve hot, garnished with parsley sprigs.

Per serving: 237 calories, 14 g protein, 1 g fat (0.1 g sat), 47 g carbs, 83 mg sodium, 216 mg calcium, 14 g fiber

Note: Analysis doesn't include salt to taste and parsley for garnish.

TIPS FROM THE TRENCHES

"The other day my husband said, 'I don't have heartburn anymore!' I knew it would happen, but I let him discover it for himself. It will mean more to him that way."

This thick, flavorful stew is hearty enough to serve as a main dish, especially if you serve it with baked tortilla chips or ladle it over cooked whole grains. Feel free to substitute vegan chicken or other plant-based proteins for the vegan prawns.

SOUTHWESTERN **fusion** STEW

MAKES 4 SERVINGS

1 cup no-salt-added **vegetable broth**

1 large **sweet yellow onion,** finely chopped

2 **red bell peppers,** thickly sliced

1 **green bell pepper,** thickly sliced

6 cloves **garlic,** finely chopped

1 can (28 ounces) no-salt-added chopped **Roma tomatoes** with liquid

1 cup low-sodium spicy **vegetable juice**

2 tablespoons dried **basil**

2 tablespoons dried **parsley**

1 teaspoon dried **dill weed**

1 teaspoon **paprika**

1 teaspoon dried **thyme**

1 teaspoon ground **turmeric**

1 **bay leaf**

Pinch **cayenne**

1 can (15 ounces) **white hominy,** drained

1 package (8.8 ounces) **vegan prawns or shrimp,** thawed if frozen (optional)

Salt

Put the broth in a large pot. Add the onion, bell peppers, and garlic and bring to a boil over high heat. Decrease the heat to medium, cover, and cook, stirring occasionally, until the onion is translucent, about 10 minutes.

Stir in the tomatoes, vegetable juice, basil, parsley, dill, paprika, thyme, turmeric, bay leaf, and cayenne. Decrease the heat to medium-low, cover, and cook, stirring occasionally, for 20 minutes.

Stir in the hominy and optional prawns, cover, and cook, stirring occasionally, for 15 minutes. Season with salt to taste. Serve hot.

Per serving: 193 calories, 6 g protein, 1 g fat (0.1 g sat), 37 g carbs, 691 mg sodium, 202 mg calcium, 10 g fiber

Note: Analysis doesn't include salt to taste.

This robust chowder has captured many a heart. It boasts all the flavor of traditional versions with none of the seafood, making it a true win-win for everyone.

bouillabaisse

4 cups **water**

4 tablespoons low-sodium **vegetable broth powder**

8 new or red **potatoes,** scrubbed and cut into bite-sized pieces

1 cup chopped **leek** (white and tender green parts only)

1 cup finely chopped **yellow onion**

3 cups chopped fresh or no-salt-added **canned tomatoes** with liquid

1 can (6 ounces) no-salt-added **tomato paste**

½ cup chopped fresh flat-leaf **parsley,** lightly packed, plus more for garnish

2 tablespoons chopped fresh **thyme,** or 2 teaspoons dried

2 **bay leaves**

2 tablespoons whole-grain **flour**

1 pound **vegan prawns or shrimp,** thawed if frozen

1 can (15 ounces) no-salt-added **garbanzo beans,** drained and rinsed

½ teaspoon **saffron**

Salt and pepper

Put the water and broth powder in a large pot and stir to combine. Add the potatoes, leek, and onion and bring to a boil over high heat. Decrease the heat to medium-low, cover, and cook, stirring occasionally, just until the vegetables are tender, about 15 minutes.

Add the tomatoes, tomato paste, parsley, thyme, and bay leaves and cook, stirring occasionally, for 10 minutes. Ladle about ½ cup of the broth into a small bowl. Stir in the flour, then stir the mixture into the soup.

Add the vegan prawns, beans, and saffron and cook, stirring occasionally, until heated through, 5 to 10 minutes. Season with salt and pepper to taste. Serve hot, garnished with parsley.

Per serving: 531 calories, 17 g protein, 1 g fat (0 g sat), 115 g carbs, 249 mg sodium, 384 mg calcium, 16 g fiber

Note: Analysis doesn't include salt to taste or additional parsley for garnish.

chapter five

SALADS FOR SOLIDARITY

Raw fresh vegetables are so healthful. They truly belong on every plate, no matter what the diner's dietary persuasion. The bountiful salads in this chapter feature ingredients that are enticing, satisfying, and, in some cases, packed with protein, elevating them far beyond the typical tossed green salad. They are a surefire way to tempt others into incorporating more plant-based foods into their diet. Many of these salads are also hearty enough to suffice as a main dish.

Even the pickiest, most vegetable-averse eaters tend to like coleslaw, making it a great common-ground dish. This version is so much better than the typical deli fare, which tends to be heavy on the mayo. I've replaced the usual sugar with dates, making for a slaw that's naturally sweet.

NATURALLY SWEET slaw

2 cups shredded **red cabbage**

2 cups shredded **green cabbage**

2 cups shredded **carrots**

½ cup finely chopped **yellow onion**

¼ cup finely chopped **soft dates,** preferably medjool

¼ cup **raisins,** finely chopped

⅓ cup **balsamic vinegar,** preferably fig-infused

1 tablespoon **caraway seeds**

1 tablespoon **Dijon mustard**

⅓ cup **olive oil** (optional)

Put the red cabbage, green cabbage, carrots, and onion in a large bowl and toss to combine. Add the dates and raisins and toss again.

Combine the vinegar, caraway seeds, and mustard in a small bowl and whisk until well blended. While whisking constantly, add the optional oil in a slow, steady stream and continue whisking until well blended. Drizzle over the cabbage mixture and toss until the vegetables are evenly coated.

Per serving: 113 calories, 2 g protein, 0.3 g fat (0 g sat), 28 g carbs, 84 mg sodium, 49 mg calcium, 4 g fiber

COLESLAW WITH CREAMY DRESSING: Replace the vinegar and optional oil with ½ cup vegan sour cream whisked with 2 tablespoons unsweetened nondairy milk. Alternatively, replace the vinegar and optional oil with ⅔ cup Creamy Caesar Dressing (page 69).

The orange, mango, and pomegranate in this salad make it so juicy and flavorful that no dressing is needed. These ingredients also provide copious vitamin C, which boosts both the immune system and mood. Although the pomegranate seeds are optional, I heartily recommend including them. In addition to being delightfully succulent, pomegranates represent abundance, marriage, and fertility in many cultures.

YOU ARE MY sunshine SALAD

10 ounces baby **spinach**

1 ripe **tomato**, preferably heirloom, chopped

4 ounces **sugar snap peas,** trimmed

1 **orange,** peeled, sectioned, and seeded

½ **mango,** cut into cubes (see tip)

½ **red bell pepper,** cut into thin strips

2 ounces **pomegranate seeds** (optional)

Combine the spinach, tomato, sugar snap peas, orange, mango, and bell pepper in a large bowl and toss gently to combine. Scatter the optional pomegranate seeds over the top.

Per serving: 74 calories, 3 g protein, 0.4 g fat (0 g sat), 16 g carbs, 103 mg sodium, 105 mg calcium, 4 g fiber

TIP: Hold the mango vertically, resting on a cutting board. With a sharp knife, cut through it lengthwise from top to bottom, cutting as close to the seed as possible without cutting into the seed. Hold the seedless side upright with one hand and cut lines across the flesh, being careful not to puncture the skin. Rotate the mango 90 degrees and cut a set of perpendicular lines. Pick up the mango half, holding in both hands with the skin facing you, and press in the center with your thumbs to push the cut cubes out, somewhat resembling a porcupine. If the mango is very ripe, the cubes may fall out; however, you'll probably need to slice along the edge of the skin to release them. Cut the seed out of the other half of the mango and repeat the procedure.

Growing a vegetable garden is a wonderful way to establish common ground, both literally and figuratively. Plus, in the height of summer, you may be able to harvest most of the ingredients for this refreshing salad from your backyard. That's both convenient and economical!

GARDEN-OF-DELIGHTS **salad**

MAKES 4 SERVINGS

4 ounces **okra,** thinly sliced

1 head **romaine** or **red leaf lettuce**

2 cups **baby arugula,** lightly packed

4 ounces cremini or button **mushrooms,** sliced

¾ cup **cherry tomatoes,** halved

½ **zucchini,** thinly sliced

½ **red bell pepper,** cut into thin strips

¼ cup chopped fresh **dill,** lightly packed

4 leaves fresh **basil,** chopped

½ cup **Balsamic Vinaigrette** (page 63)

Put the okra in a small pot and add water to cover generously. Bring to a boil over high heat. Decrease the heat to medium-low, cover, and cook until the okra is tender, about 20 minutes. Drain, rinse, and then drain well. Let cool to room temperature.

Tear the lettuce into bite-sized pieces and put it in a large salad bowl or on a large platter. Add the arugula and toss to combine. Place the mushrooms and tomatoes around the perimeter. Put the okra, zucchini, and bell pepper in the center. Sprinkle the dill and basil over the top, then drizzle evenly with the vinaigrette.

Per serving: 181 calories, 3 g protein, 15 g fat (2 g sat), 12 g carbs, 222 mg sodium, 75 mg calcium, 3 g fiber

A headline grabber when served on its own or when paired with a main dish, this salad is totally satisfying. Brilliant green baby spinach leaves make a stunning bed for a tasty combination of artichoke hearts and beans dressed in a flavorful sour cream sauce.

spinach SALAD WITH ARTICHOKES AND GARBANZOS

1 container (8 ounces) vegan **sour cream**

½ cup **salsa**

Juice of 1 **lemon**

3 tablespoons low-sodium **vegetable broth powder**

1 can (15 ounces) no-salt-added **garbanzo beans,** drained and rinsed

1 can (about 14 ounces) water-packed **artichoke hearts,** drained and quartered

2 **green onions,** cut diagonally into ½-inch pieces

10 ounces **baby spinach**

Put the vegan sour cream, salsa, lemon juice, and vegetable broth powder in a large bowl and stir to combine. Fold in the beans, artichokes, and half of the green onions. Line a serving dish with the spinach. Mound the bean mixture in the center and garnish with the remaining green onion.

Per serving: 307 calories, 9 g protein, 10 g fat (4 g sat), 46 g carbs, 557 mg sodium, 128 mg calcium, 7 g fiber

TIPS FROM THE TRENCHES

"A good way to compromise is to make a vegan meal, with those who choose to eat meat either adding it to their portion or eating it on the side. Potluck-style dinners, with each person contributing a different dish, work well if there are several people in the group."

This salad is a crowd-pleaser, and for good reason: with its wide variety of ingredients, it definitely has something for everyone. And because it has so many ingredients, you can easily leave out any that aren't popular in your household. Sprinkling nuts and seeds on anything green, as with the pistachios and sunflower seeds in this recipe, is a great way to coax others to try more vegetables.

SOMETHING-FOR-**everyone** SALAD

MAKES 4 SERVINGS

½ cup freshly squeezed **lemon juice**

¼ cup **water**

2 ripe **avocados,** sliced

1 head red leaf, Boston, or Bibb **lettuce,** or a combination

2 ripe **tomatoes,** cut into thick wedges

¾ cup shredded **red cabbage**

½ **red onion,** cut into thin rings

½ **yellow bell pepper,** cut into thin strips

¼ cup pitted **black olives,** sliced

½ bunch **watercress,** trimmed

2 tablespoons chopped fresh flat-leaf **parsley**

¼ cup unsalted **pistachio nuts**

¼ cup raw or unsalted roasted **sunflower seeds**

1 cup **alfalfa sprouts**

½ cup **Lemon-Dill Dressing** (page 62)

Mix the lemon juice and water in a small bowl. Briefly dip the avocado slices into the lemon juice mixture to prevent browning.

Line a large plate with the lettuce, completely covering the plate. (If using lettuce with various colors, alternate them for more eye appeal.) Arrange the tomatoes, cabbage, onion, and bell pepper around the edges, alternating them to create a colorful effect and spiraling them toward the center.

Sprinkle the olives over the vegetables. Scatter the watercress and parsley over the top. Sprinkle with the pistachios and sunflower seeds. Place the sprouts in a cluster in the center. Drizzle evenly with the dressing.

Per serving: 402 calories, 9 g protein, 33 g fat (4 g sat), 26 g carbs, 136 mg sodium, 161 mg calcium, 13 g fiber

TIP: Be aware that nuts and seeds are calorie-dense and therefore should be used in moderate amounts.

If you're still trying to please everyone all the time, here's a salad that just might do the trick. Think of the recipe as a template and tweak the ingredients to appeal to the non-vegans in your household. Simply offer all the prepared ingredients in individual bowls and allow everyone to assemble their own salad.

please 'em all SALAD BAR

1 head romaine **lettuce,** torn

2 ripe **tomatoes,** cut into thick wedges

2 **carrots,** cut into thin rounds or half-moons

1 **beet,** peeled and shredded

½ **cucumber,** cut into thin rounds or half-moons

8 small **broccoli florets**

8 small **cauliflower florets**

½ small **zucchini,** cut into thin rounds or matchsticks

½ cup no-salt-added cooked or canned **garbanzo beans,** drained and rinsed

½ cup no-salt-added cooked or canned **kidney beans,** drained and rinsed

½ cup shredded vegan **Cheddar cheese**

½ cup pitted **olives,** sliced

4 **mushrooms,** sliced

¼ **red onion,** cut into thin half-moons

¼ cup chopped **walnuts**

¼ cup **raisins**

Various **salad dressings** (optional)

Put all the ingredients in individual bowls and allow everyone to assemble and dress their own salad as desired.

Per serving: 292 calories, 10 g protein, 12 g fat (2 g sat), 39 g carbs, 330 mg sodium, 90 mg calcium, 11 g fiber
Note: Analyzed with Daiya Cheddar-style shreds.

TIP: To speed preparation, you can slice most of the vegetables in a food processor if you like.

Caprese salad has become so popular. Here's a version that amps up the flavor with red onion and kalamata olives and forgoes the saturated fat in fresh mozzarella. Plus, this recipe doesn't call for arranging the components on a platter, which can be time-consuming. Though the process is streamlined, the final results remain elegant.

caprese SALAD

4 large ripe **tomatoes,** preferably heirloom, halved vertically, then thickly sliced

1 small **red onion,** thinly sliced

2 cups fresh **basil leaves,** lightly packed

12 pitted **kalamata olives,** chopped

4 teaspoons **balsamic vinegar**

2 teaspoons chopped fresh flat-leaf **parsley**

1 teaspoon **olive oil** (optional)

Salt

Ground **pepper**

1 cup shredded **vegan cheese,** any variety

Put the tomatoes and onion in a large bowl and stir gently to combine. Add the basil, olives, vinegar, parsley, and optional oil and stir again until evenly combined. Cover and refrigerate for at least 1 hour, until well chilled and the flavors have melded. Just before serving, season with salt and pepper to taste and sprinkle with the vegan cheese.

Per serving: 163 calories, 3 g protein, 9 g fat (2 g sat), 18 g carbs, 370 mg sodium, 63 mg calcium, 4 g fiber

Note: Analyzed with Daiya mozzarella-style shreds. Analysis doesn't include salt to taste.

Good-as-Gold Soup, *page 32*

Overstuffed Soft Tacos, *page 80*

This satisfying salad provides plenty of protein. The tempeh has a meaty texture and savory flavor that will be a pleasant surprise to those who thought they didn't care for soy foods.

SPINACH **salad** WITH TEMPEH AND CREAMY TARRAGON DRESSING

MAKES 4 SERVINGS

1 package (8 ounces) **tempeh,** cut into narrow strips lengthwise

¼ cup reduced-sodium **soy sauce**

10 ounces **baby spinach**

1½ cups **cherry tomatoes,** halved

1 package (12 ounces) frozen **artichoke hearts,** thawed and drained (optional)

1 cup frozen **petite peas,** thawed and drained

2 **green onions,** cut diagonally into ½-inch pieces

1 cup **Creamy Tarragon Dressing** (page 70)

Put the tempeh in a medium nonstick skillet over medium heat. Drizzle with the soy sauce and turn to coat. Cook without turning until crispy on the bottom, about 10 minutes. Flip and cook until the other side is crispy, about 10 minutes. Let cool slightly.

Put the spinach, tomatoes, optional artichoke hearts, peas, and green onions in a large shallow bowl and toss gently to combine. Drizzle with the dressing and toss again until all the ingredients are evenly coated. Place the tempeh atop the salad, arranging it like the spokes of a wheel.

Per serving: 161 calories, 18 g protein, 12 g fat (3 g sat), 18 g carbs, 587 mg sodium, 160 mg calcium, 5 g fiber

If you have cooked millet on hand, you can put this attractive composed salad together fairly quickly—and without heating up the kitchen, which is a real boon when the weather is hot. Although I've classified it as a salad in this book, it's hearty enough to serve as a main dish.

composed TOMATO AND MILLET SALAD

MAKES 4 SERVINGS

4 large leaves **romaine lettuce**

2 cups cooked **millet** (see page 11)

4 large ripe **tomatoes,** halved vertically

1 **red onion,** cut into thin rounds

1 **cucumber,** cut into ¼-inch-thick rounds

1 **yellow summer squash,** cut into
   ¼-inch-thick rounds

1 roasted **red bell pepper,** cut into 8 pieces

1 can (15 ounces) no-salt-added **garbanzo
   beans,** drained and rinsed

1 cup pitted **kalamata** or other black olives,
   sliced

¼ cup chopped fresh **basil,** lightly packed

3 tablespoons chopped fresh **chives**

3 tablespoons chopped fresh **cilantro**

1 tablespoon **olive oil** (optional)

1 teaspoon balsamic **vinegar**

To compose each serving, put 1 leaf of the lettuce on a salad plate. Top each leaf with ½ cup of the millet, then position the 2 halves of a tomato atop the millet, cut-side up.

Arrange the onion, cucumber, and yellow squash around the tomatoes, overlapping the ingredients as needed and fitting the cucumber and squash within the onion rings. Put a piece of bell pepper on top of each tomato half.

Scatter the beans and olives around the plate, then sprinkle with the basil, chives, and cilantro. Drizzle evenly with the optional oil and the vinegar.

Per serving: 342 calories, 12 g protein, 8 g fat (1 g sat), 56 g carbs, 446 mg sodium, 154 mg calcium, 10 g fiber

Quinoa has more protein per serving than any other grain. In this salad, I've combined it with edamame for a one-two protein punch. Best of all, this salad gets more flavorful with time, making it great to keep on hand for those times when hunger strikes but you're too busy to cook.

LEMONY QUINOA **tabouli**

¾ cup shelled fresh (see tip) or frozen **edamame**

2 cups cooked **quinoa** (see page 11), at room temperature

2 large ripe **tomatoes,** chopped

1 **cucumber,** chopped

1 cup chopped fresh **parsley,** lightly packed

½ cup chopped fresh **mint,** lightly packed

⅓ cup thinly sliced **green onions**

¼ cup sliced **almonds**

2 tablespoons **sesame seeds**

¾ cup **Lemon-Dill Dressing** (page 62)

Salt

Ground **pepper**

Bring a small pot of water to a boil over high heat. Add the edamame. Return to a boil, decrease the heat to medium, and cook until tender, about 5 minutes. Drain, then rinse with cold water.

To assemble the salad, put the edamame, quinoa, tomatoes, cucumber, parsley, mint, green onions, almonds, and sesame seeds in a large bowl and toss with two forks to combine. Drizzle with the dressing and toss again until all the ingredients are evenly coated. Season with salt and pepper to taste.

Cover and refrigerate for at least 1 hour, until well chilled. Serve cold or at room temperature. Stored in a sealed container in the refrigerator, the salad will keep for 5 days.

Per serving: 386 calories, 12 g protein, 23 g fat (2 g sat), 33 g carbs, 29 mg sodium, 115 mg calcium, 10 g fiber

Note: Analysis doesn't include salt to taste.

TIP: If the edamame you're using is precooked, there is no need to boil it; that step of the recipe may be skipped.

Whole grains are so healthful, yet many people struggle to find creative ways to incorporate them into menus. Grain-based salads are a perfect solution-satisfying, versatile, and, once assembled, oh-so-convenient. After the rice is cooked, this salad is a snap to put together, especially if you use a food processor to slice the vegetables.

RICE SALAD **dijon**

4 cups cooked **brown rice** (see page 11), at room temperature

1 cup **Dijon Vinaigrette** (page 64), plus more if desired

10 ounces frozen **peas,** thawed

1 **red bell pepper,** cut into thin strips

1 **yellow bell pepper,** cut into thin strips

1 **carrot,** cut into thin rounds

6 **green onions,** thinly sliced

1 cup **raisins**

¼ cup sliced **almonds** or unsalted **pistachio nuts**

¼ cup chopped fresh **dill,** lightly packed, or 4 teaspoons dried dill weed

¼ cup chopped fresh **parsley,** lightly packed

Put the rice in a large bowl. Drizzle with the vinaigrette and toss with two forks until the rice is evenly coated. Add the peas, bell peppers, carrot, green onions, raisins, almonds, dill, and parsley. Toss again until all the ingredients are evenly coated with the vinaigrette. Stored in a sealed container in the refrigerator, the salad will keep for 5 days.

Per serving: 358 calories, 9 g protein, 5 g fat (0.4 g sat), 67 g carbs, 110 mg sodium, 81 mg calcium, 10 g fiber

RICE AND BEAN SALAD DIJON: For even more protein, add 1 can (15 ounces) of no-salt-added beans, drained and rinsed. Garbanzo beans or black beans would be especially tasty in this dish.

This is a great refrigerator staple to have on hand, fueling you in a pinch if you're scrambling to feed everyone else. And not that I recommend dissembling, but this salad is so tasty and authentic that nonvegans may not be able to tell it isn't the "real" thing.

stealth EGG SALAD

1 pound **firm tofu,** preferably silken, drained

½ cup chopped **celery**

½ cup finely chopped fresh **dill,** lightly packed

½ cup finely chopped **red onion**

¼ cup vegan **mayonnaise**

2 tablespoons chopped fresh **chives** (optional)

2 tablespoons **dill relish** or finely chopped **dill pickle**

4 teaspoons **Dijon mustard**

4 teaspoons reduced-sodium **soy sauce**

1 tablespoon **capers** (optional)

2 teaspoons ground **turmeric**

½ teaspoon **garlic powder**

Put the tofu in a large bowl and mash it with a fork, leaving a few larger chunks for texture. Add the celery, dill, onion, vegan mayonnaise, optional chives, relish, mustard, soy sauce, optional capers, turmeric, and garlic powder and stir to combine. Stored in a sealed container in the refrigerator, the salad will keep for 5 days.

Per serving: 171 calories, 11 g protein, 11 g fat (1 g sat), 7 g carbs, 393 mg sodium, 170 mg calcium, 2 g fiber

This salad breaks with tradition, replacing fish with baked tofu. The secret to great baked tofu is in the marinade, and this one's a winner!

MAKE-NICE **niçoise** SALAD

MAKES 4 SERVINGS

BAKED TOFU

1 pound **extra-firm tofu,** drained

¼ cup **hoisin sauce**

¼ cup reduced-sodium **soy sauce**

1 tablespoon **paprika**

½ teaspoon ground **ginger**

1 clove **garlic,** chopped

SALAD

4 small **red potatoes,** scrubbed

1 pound fresh **green beans,** trimmed, or frozen green beans

4 ripe **Roma tomatoes,** quartered

½ small **red onion,** cut into thin half-moons

1 roasted **red bell pepper,** cut into thin strips

¼ cup pitted **Greek olives**

2 tablespoons finely chopped fresh flat-leaf **parsley**

½ teaspoon ground **pepper**

⅔ cup **Dijon Vinaigrette** (page 64)

Per serving: 435 calories, 26 g protein, 15 g fat (3 g sat), 53 g carbs, 676 mg sodium, 755 mg calcium, 10 g fiber

To make the baked tofu, put the tofu in a shallow pan and place a heavy plate on top. Let sit for at least 30 minutes to press out excess moisture.

Slice the tofu crosswise into 8 equal pieces. Put the hoisin sauce, soy sauce, paprika, ginger, and garlic in a shallow pan and whisk to combine. Add the tofu and turn to coat. Cover and refrigerate for at least 2 hours or up to 24 hours, turning the tofu occasionally.

Preheat the oven to 350 degrees F. Line a rimmed baking sheet with parchment paper or mist it with cooking spray.

Put the tofu on the lined baking sheet in a single layer. Bake for 20 minutes, then gently turn it over and bake for about 20 minutes longer, until crisp around the edges. Let cool, then cut into cubes.

Meanwhile, to make the salad, put the potatoes in a medium pot and add water to cover generously. Bring to a boil over high heat. Decrease the heat to medium, cover partially, and cook just until tender, about 15 minutes. Drain well and transfer to a large bowl to cool.

Rinse the pot in which the potatoes were cooked. Pour in ½ inch of water, then add the green beans. Bring to a boil over high heat. Decrease the heat to medium, cover, and cook until the green beans are tender, 8 to 10 minutes. Drain well.

When the potatoes are cool enough to handle, cut them into large pieces. Transfer to a large bowl. Add the tofu, green beans, tomatoes, onion, bell pepper, olives, parsley, and pepper and stir gently to combine. Drizzle with the dressing and stir gently until all the ingredients are evenly coated. Stored in a sealed container in the refrigerator, the salad will keep for 5 days.

This salad is a delight as is or atop a bed of fresh greens. As a bonus, the flavors develop and meld with time, so leftovers are even tastier.

go-to GARBANZO SALAD

2 tablespoons **olive oil, vegetable broth, or water**

1/2 cup chopped **yellow onion**

1/2 cup chopped **red cabbage**

2 tablespoons chopped fresh **thyme,** or 2 teaspoons dried

1/2 cup chopped **red bell pepper**

2 cans (15 ounces each) no-salt-added **garbanzo beans,** drained and rinsed

1/3 cup **raisins** (optional)

1/3 cup balsamic **vinegar,** preferably fig-infused

Heat the oil in a large saucepan over medium-low heat. Add the onion, cabbage, and thyme and cook, stirring occasionally, until the onion is tender, about 10 minutes.

Add the bell pepper and cook, stirring occasionally, for 5 minutes. Add the beans and optional raisins and cook, stirring occasionally, just until heated through, about 5 minutes. Transfer to a large bowl. Drizzle with the vinegar and stir gently until evenly distributed.

Let cool to room temperature, then cover and refrigerate for at least 2 hours before serving. Stored in a sealed container in the refrigerator, the salad will keep for 5 days.

Per serving: 300 calories, 12 g protein, 8 g fat (1 g sat), 46 g carbs, 57 mg sodium, 110 mg calcium, 9 g fiber

chapter six

HARMONIZING DRESSINGS, MARINADES, AND SAUCES

When you're living with a kitchen divided, sharing certain foods can help ease tensions and make meal preparation easier. I recommend that you try all the recipes in this chapter to determine which ones are the most popular in your household. Then keep a few of the dressings and sauces in your refrigerator at all times to facilitate whipping up last-minute dishes. After all, often the most complicated part of cooking is seasoning a dish. Having dressings, marinades, and sauces ready to go will take away the guesswork and infuse your food with tried-and-true flavor combinations that everyone will love. Many of the following recipes can be used as a straightforward dressing for a salad; as a topping or seasoning for grains, greens, or beans; or as a marinade for plant-based meat alternatives (or, if others insist, for meat). And because these recipes keep well, having several on hand will not only be convenient, but it will also make customizing dishes to suit individual tastes a snap.

This simple yet zippy salad dressing has universal appeal.

lemon-dill DRESSING

MAKES ABOUT ¾ CUP

½ cup freshly squeezed **lemon juice**

1 tablespoon chopped fresh **dill,** or
   1 teaspoon dried dill weed

½ teaspoon **garlic powder**

¼ cup **olive oil**

Put the lemon juice, dill, and garlic powder in a small bowl and whisk to combine. Add the oil and whisk until thoroughly blended. Stored in a sealed container in the refrigerator, the dressing will keep for 2 weeks.

Per 2 tablespoons: 87 calories, 0 g protein, 9 g fat (1 g sat), 2 g carbs, 3 mg sodium, 10 mg calcium, 0 g fiber

TIPS FROM THE TRENCHES

"It's important to have an open, honest discussion about how you feel and also to have resources, such as documentaries and books, to show how the meat and dairy industries function. Don't badger a partner who eats meat; that usually just makes matters worse. Instead, invite your partner to cook with you and help her (or him) discover the joys of vegan eating."

This basic balsamic vinaigrette will rev up any salad with its delicate balance of spices.

BALSAMIC **vinaigrette**

¼ cup **balsamic vinegar**

2 teaspoons reduced-sodium **soy sauce**

½ teaspoon **celery salt**

¼ teaspoon dried **basil**

¼ teaspoon dried **dill weed**

¼ teaspoon dried **mint**

¼ teaspoon dried **oregano**

⅛ teaspoon **garlic powder**

⅛ teaspoon ground **pepper**

5 tablespoons **olive oil** or no-salt-added **vegetable broth**

Put the vinegar, soy sauce, celery salt, basil, dill, mint, oregano, garlic powder, and pepper in a small bowl and whisk to combine. Add the oil and whisk until thoroughly blended. Stored in a sealed container in the refrigerator, the vinaigrette will keep for 2 weeks.

Per 2 tablespoons: 130 calories, 0 g protein, 14 g fat (2 g sat), 3 g carbs, 211 mg sodium, 4 mg calcium, 0 g fiber

TIP: For an even lighter, totally fat-free version, use the vegetable broth option instead of the olive oil.

In addition to being wonderful on salads (see Rice Salad Dijon, page 56), this flavor-packed vinaigrette works well as a marinade for baked tofu (see Make-Nice Niçoise Salad, page 58).

dijon VINAIGRETTE OR MARINADE

MAKES ABOUT 2½ CUPS

1 cup **water**

½ cup raw or unsalted roasted **almonds**

¼ cup chopped fresh **chives**

¼ cup chopped fresh **parsley,** lightly packed

¼ cup **red wine vinegar**

2 pitted **soft dates,** preferably medjool

2 tablespoons **Dijon mustard**

½ teaspoon ground **pepper**

Put all the ingredients in a blender and process until smooth. Stored in a sealed container in the refrigerator, the vinaigrette will keep for 2 weeks.

Per 2 tablespoons: 26 calories, 1 g protein, 1 g fat (0.2 g sat), 3 g carbs, 35 mg sodium, 14 mg calcium, 1 g fiber

GARLICKY DIJON VINAIGRETTE: Add 6 cloves of garlic, chopped, and omit the almonds and dates.

This recipe is a rich-tasting yet fat-free spin on French dressing. I recommend using it untraditionally, such as on Mexican fare. It's terrific on a taco salad or as a marinade for plant-based proteins to be used in fillings for burritos or enchiladas.

tomato DRESSING OR MARINADE

MAKES ABOUT 3¼ CUPS

- 1 can (15 ounces) no-salt-added **tomato sauce**
- 1 cup **apple cider vinegar**
- 4 pitted **soft dates,** preferably medjool
- 1 tablespoon dried **onion flakes**
- 1 teaspoon **celery seed**
- 1 teaspoon **garlic powder**
- 1 teaspoon **paprika**

Put all the ingredients in a blender and process until smooth. Stored in a sealed container in the refrigerator, the dressing will keep for 2 weeks.

Per 2 tablespoons: 19 calories, 1 g protein, 0 g fat (0 g sat), 4 g carbs, 3 mg sodium, 4 mg calcium, 1 g fiber

TIPS FROM THE TRENCHES

"I'm vegan and my husband is vegetarian at home. When we go out, sometimes he orders meat, but I don't get mad at him. We mostly cook and eat at home, so we get lots of veggies, grains, beans, and fruits. He loves seitan, and we typically use that in place of meat. He's a really good cook, and we love to experiment with cooking different vegan foods together. I knew he was a keeper when I went to his house on our second date and he opened the pantry to show me all the vegan items he'd bought. Before we got married, we had a discussion about how we would raise our children. He said he had no problem raising our children vegan."

Sprightly on salads, this tropical-infused delight is also a fantastic marinade for tofu, tempeh, and many other plant-based foods.

citrus-mango DRESSING OR MARINADE

2 **oranges,** peeled, sectioned, and seeded

1 fresh **mango,** cut into large pieces (see tip, page 47), or 8 ounces frozen mango chunks

¼ cup **raisins** or chopped soft dates, preferably medjool

6 sprigs **parsley**

1 tablespoon chopped fresh **basil,** or 1 teaspoon dried

1 tablespoon reduced-sodium **soy sauce**

3 cloves **garlic**

1 piece (¼ inch) fresh **ginger**

Put all the ingredients in a blender and process until smooth. Stored in a sealed container in the refrigerator, the dressing will keep for 5 days.

Per 2 tablespoons: 18 calories, 0 g protein, 0 g fat (0 g sat), 5 g carbs, 33 mg sodium, 7 mg calcium, 1 g fiber

Try this dressing on steamed asparagus or very thinly sliced vegetables, or use it as a marinade for plant-based proteins before adding them to Asian dishes.

asian DRESSING OR MARINADE

1 **orange,** peeled, sectioned, and seeded

¼ cup reduced-sodium **soy sauce**

2 tablespoons **hoisin sauce**

1 teaspoon ground **ginger,** or 1 piece (1½ inches) fresh ginger

1 clove **garlic,** chopped

Put all the ingredients in a blender and process until smooth. Stored in a sealed container in the refrigerator, the dressing will keep for 5 days.

Per 2 tablespoons: 22 calories, 1 g protein, 0.2 g fat (0.1 g sat), 5 g carbs, 354 mg sodium, 7 mg calcium, 1 g fiber

TIPS FROM THE TRENCHES

"My husband and I do very well in our 'mixed marriage.' I compare it to a household with different religious views where both mates respect the other's right to choose. I don't cook meat for him; if he wants meat, he cooks it himself. I make many flexible meals that can be served with or without meat. And since I became vegan, he's been eating many more whole grains, veggies, and fruits."

Sweet, sour, salty, and spicy—this dressing has it all. Use it anytime you want to amp up the flavor of veggies, beans, and almost everything else!

anything-goes DRESSING OR MARINADE

4 pitted **soft dates,** preferably medjool

¼ cup pitted **olives,** chopped

¼ cup **red wine vinegar**

2 tablespoons plain **nondairy yogurt,** plus more if desired

4 teaspoons **capers**

1 tablespoon **Dijon mustard**

2 cloves **garlic**

1 teaspoon vegan **red chili paste**

Put all the ingredients in a blender and process until smooth. For a thinner dressing, add up to 2 tablespoons more non-dairy yogurt. Stored in a sealed container in the refrigerator, the dressing will keep for 5 days.

Per 2 tablespoons: 44 calories, 1 g protein, 0.4 g fat (0 g sat), 111 g carbs, 96 mg sodium, 15 mg calcium, 1 g fiber

Note: Analyzed with plain soy yogurt.

TIPS FROM THE TRENCHES

"My family is very respectful and usually eats what I make for them, though my daughter sometimes gets a little frustrated. Thankfully, my husband only eats meat if he's out, and he never brings any home."

Vegan mayonnaise may not rank high on any list of healthful foods, but it can be a great transition ingredient. Some folks will eat just about anything if it's doused in a creamy, mayo-based dressing, especially one that's spiked with lemon juice and garlic, as is this recipe.

CREAMY caesar DRESSING

1 cup vegan **mayonnaise**

¾ cup vegan **Parmesan cheese** (see page 12)

Juice of 2 **lemons**

¼ cup **water**

2 tablespoons vegan **Worcestershire sauce**

¼ teaspoon **garlic powder,** or 2 cloves garlic, finely chopped

Put all the ingredients in a blender and process until well blended. Alternatively, combine the ingredients in a bowl and whisk until well blended. Stored in a sealed container in the refrigerator, the dressing will keep for 7 days.

Per 2 tablespoons: 98 calories, 2 g protein, 8 g fat (0.4 g sat), 2 g carbs, 134 mg sodium, 40 mg calcium, 1 g fiber

Note: Analyzed with Galaxy Nutritional Foods parmesan-flavored topping.

CREAMY CAESAR MARINADE: For a creamy marinade that's great for infusing plain or seasoned seitan with an extra jolt of flavor, stir in another ¼ cup of water.

This fragrant, creamy, tarragon-infused dressing will enhance almost any salad, or use it as a sauce over faux (or genuine) seafood.

CREAMY **tarragon** DRESSING OR SAUCE

6 ounces **silken tofu,** drained

⅓ cup **tarragon mustard** or **Dijon mustard**

⅓ cup **olive oil**

¼ cup **tarragon vinegar** or fig-infused balsamic vinegar

1 teaspoon dried **tarragon**

Salt

Ground **pepper**

Put the tofu, mustard, oil, vinegar, and tarragon in a blender and process until smooth. Season with salt and pepper to taste. Stored in a sealed container in the refrigerator, the dressing will keep for 5 days.

Per 2 tablespoons: 56 calories, 1 g protein, 5 g fat (1 g sat), 0 g carbs, 130 mg sodium, 3 mg calcium, 0 g fiber

Note: Analysis doesn't include salt to taste.

LOW-FAT CREAMY TARRAGON DRESSING OR SAUCE: Substitute no-salt-added vegan chicken broth or water for the olive oil.

Perfect for salads or as a topping for baked tofu, tempeh, or other meat alternatives, this sauce is also wonderful on vegan seafood, such as vegan prawns.

creamy DILL-MUSTARD DRESSING OR SAUCE

MAKES ABOUT 2 CUPS

¾ cup vegan **sour cream**

4 ounces **silken tofu,** drained

1 **lemon** or **lime,** peeled, halved crosswise, and seeded

¼ cup chopped fresh **dill,** lightly packed, or 4 teaspoons dried dill weed

1 **green onion**

1 tablespoon **Dijon mustard**

2 teaspoons reduced-sodium **soy sauce**

1 clove **garlic,** chopped

Put all the ingredients in a blender and process until well blended. Stored in a sealed container in the refrigerator, the dressing will keep for 5 days.

Per 2 tablespoons: 36 calories, 1 g protein, 3 g fat (1 g sat), 3 g carbs, 68 mg sodium, 35 mg calcium, 1 g fiber

TIPS FROM THE TRENCHES

"Don't say a word about diet. Just cook and present delicious, delightful foods. Don't get into any arguments about not having meat, and don't expect any kudos—at least not at first."

Mushroom sauces are so versatile and have seemingly endless uses. Almost any savory dish, particularly those containing whole grains or pasta, will become instantly more delectable when doused in this version.

CREAMY **mushroom** SAUCE

MAKES ABOUT 2½ CUPS

1 cup **water**

1 cup thinly sliced **mushrooms,** such as cremini, portobello, porcini, shiitake, or a combination (see tips)

½ cup chopped **sweet onion**

2 **green onions,** thinly sliced

4 cloves **garlic,** chopped

⅓ cup light **coconut milk**

1 tablespoon low-sodium **vegetable broth powder**

¼ teaspoon ground **nutmeg** (optional)

Put the water in a large skillet, then add the mushrooms, sweet onion, green onions, and garlic. Bring to a boil over high heat. Decrease the heat to medium-low and stir in the coconut milk, broth powder, and optional nutmeg. Cook, stirring occasionally, until the mushrooms begin to soften, about 5 minutes.

Stir in the parsley and soy sauce and cook until the mushrooms are tender, about 5 minutes. Serve immediately.

Per ¼ cup: 20 calories, 1 g protein, 1 g fat (0.4 g sat), 3 g carbs, 159 mg sodium, 7 mg calcium, 1 g fiber

½ cup chopped fresh flat-leaf **parsley,** lightly packed

1 tablespoon reduced-sodium **soy sauce**

TIPS

- For a less creamy consistency, omit the coconut milk.
- For a thicker consistency, add up to 2 tablespoons of whole-grain flour when you add the soy sauce, stirring constantly as you add the flour to prevent lumps.
- You can replace the fresh mushrooms with dried mushrooms for a richer, deeper flavor. Put about ½ ounce of dried mushrooms in a bowl and add boiling water to cover generously. Put a plate or smaller bowl on top of the mushrooms to keep them submerged. Let sit until tender; the time will vary depending on the mushrooms, but about 20 minutes should suffice for most varieties. Drain well before using. You might want to save the flavorful mushroom soaking water to use as broth; if you do, strain it through a coffee filter to remove any grit.

TIPS FROM THE TRENCHES

"'One thing I don't miss is that heavy, overstuffed feeling.' When my husband finally said that, I did a little dance inside. For the win!"

chapter seven

MEET-IN-THE-MIDDLE MAIN DISHES

Main dishes are often the most contentious course in a divided kitchen. Those not of the vegan persuasion tend to believe that meat or a meat-based dish should occupy the center of the plate. Perhaps you have chosen to compromise, allowing others to cook meat or add it to main dishes. If so, you could find yourself vying for space in the kitchen, or worse, you may have to accept seeing and smelling animal products. As ever, often the best defense is a good offense. Look for opportunities to craft vegan versions of dishes that are favorites in your household. Alluring aromas can win hearts and minds (and stomachs!), and an attractive presentation is always a bonus. With time, perhaps others will begin to forgo the meat and find satisfaction in the delicious creations you've concocted.

Ah, the ubiquitous veggie stir-fry. For many people, such a dish is synonymous with vegan fare. Here, sunflower and sesame seeds provide an appealing crunch that sets this rendition apart. For more heft, feel free to include any plant-based proteins that strike your fancy.

TOSS-IT-TOGETHER **stir-fry**

MAKES 4 SERVINGS

¼ cup **water,** plus more as needed

1½ teaspoons low-sodium **vegetable broth powder**

4 ounces **mushrooms,** any variety, thinly sliced

1 **carrot,** thinly sliced

1 small **zucchini,** quartered lengthwise and then quartered crosswise

1 cup shredded **red cabbage**

1 cup cut fresh or frozen **green beans**

1 cup stemmed and chopped **kale,** lightly packed

2 **green onions,** thinly sliced

1 clove **garlic,** chopped

4 ounces **snow peas,** trimmed

1 can (8 ounces) sliced **water chestnuts,** drained

1 tablespoon reduced-sodium **soy sauce**

1 teaspoon **tahini**

1 tablespoon unsalted roasted **sunflower seeds**

1 tablespoon **sesame seeds**

2 cups cooked **brown rice** or **quinoa** (see page 11), kept hot

Put the water and broth powder in a wok or large, deep skillet and stir to combine. Add the mushrooms, carrot, zucchini, cabbage, green beans, kale, green onions, and garlic. Cook over medium-high heat, stirring frequently and adding more water as needed to prevent sticking, until the vegetables begin to soften, about 5 minutes.

Decrease the heat to medium and stir in the snow peas and water chestnuts. Put the soy sauce and tahini in a small bowl, stir to combine, then pour the mixture into the wok. Decrease the heat to low and cook, stirring gently, until the vegetables are evenly coated and the snow peas are bright green and just beginning to soften, about 3 minutes.

Remove from the heat, sprinkle with the sunflower and sesame seeds, and stir gently to combine. Serve immediately over the hot rice.

Per serving: 219 calories, 8 g protein, 4 g fat (1 g sat), 41 g carbs, 159 mg sodium, 118 mg calcium, 8 g fiber

The spices in this recipe can be toned down or revved up as you wish. Feel free to substitute other plant-based proteins, such as tempeh or seitan, for the tofu.

tofu PAD THAI

6 ounces wide **rice noodles**

1¼ cups no-salt-added **vegetable broth,** plus more as needed

¼ cup reduced-sodium **soy sauce**

3 tablespoons no-salt-added **tomato paste**

Juice of 1 **lime**

2 tablespoons vegan **red chili paste**

1 tablespoon **rice vinegar**

1 **jalapeño chile,** seeded and finely chopped

1 **onion,** chopped

2 cloves **garlic,** chopped

12 ounces **extra-firm tofu,** cut into small cubes

½ cup chopped fresh **cilantro,** lightly packed

¼ cup chopped unsalted roasted **peanuts**

1 head **romaine lettuce,** cut into thin strips

Bring a large pot of water to a boil. Turn off the heat and stir in the rice noodles. Cover and let soak, stirring occasionally, until pliable but still somewhat firm, about 10 minutes. Drain well.

Put 1 cup of the broth and the soy sauce, tomato paste, lime juice, chili paste, rice vinegar, and chile in a small bowl and stir to combine.

Put the remaining ¼ cup of broth in a wok or large non-stick skillet, then add the onion and garlic. Cook over medium heat, stirring occasionally and adding more broth as needed to prevent sticking, until the onion is translucent, about 10 minutes.

Add the tofu and cook, stirring gently, for about 5 minutes. Add the soy sauce mixture and cook, stirring gently, until the tofu has absorbed the sauce well, about 3 minutes. Add the rice noodles, cilantro, and peanuts and toss gently until the noodles are coated with the sauce and heated through, about 2 minutes.

Arrange the lettuce on a serving platter or individual plates. Spoon the noodle mixture over the lettuce. Serve immediately.

Per serving: 408 calories, 22 g protein, 14 g fat (2 g sat), 47 g carbs, 818 mg sodium, 159 mg calcium, 3 g fiber

With its fusion of Thai and Indian seasonings, this dish is akin to the Massaman curries served in most Thai restaurants. Some restaurants form the rice in heart-shaped molds and then turn it upside down onto serving plates. If you're trying to win someone over, what a great way to show your love!

SOME-LIKE-IT-HOT curry

MAKES 4 SERVINGS

¾ cup **light coconut milk**

1 **yellow onion,** chopped

3 cloves **garlic,** finely chopped

1 teaspoon finely chopped fresh **ginger**

1 teaspoon **curry powder**

½ teaspoon ground **turmeric**

Pinch **cayenne**

3 cups chopped fresh or no-salt-added **canned tomatoes** with liquid

1 tablespoon finely chopped **soft date,** preferably medjool (optional)

6 ounces **baby spinach**

1 can (15 ounces) no-salt-added **garbanzo beans,** drained and rinsed

1 cup chopped **broccoli florets**

1 cup chopped **cauliflower florets**

1 teaspoon **garam masala** (see tip)

2 cups cooked **long-grain brown rice** or **forbidden black rice** (see page 11), kept hot

Put the coconut milk in a wok or large skillet. Add the onion, garlic, ginger, curry powder, turmeric, and cayenne and cook over medium heat, stirring frequently, for 2 minutes. Stir in the tomatoes and optional date. Decrease the heat to medium-low and cook, stirring occasionally, for 10 minutes.

Stir in the spinach, beans, broccoli, cauliflower, and garam masala. Cover and cook, stirring occasionally, until the vegetables are tender, about 10 minutes. Serve over the hot rice.

Per serving: 312 calories, 12 g protein, 5 g fat (3 g sat), 55 g carbs, 84 mg sodium, 129 mg calcium, 10 g fiber

TIP: Garam masala is an Indian spice blend. Like curry powder, its ingredients vary from region to region, and it can be spicy. Look for it at Indian markets or at any store with a good selection of spices. I recommend trying a few different varieties to discover which you prefer.

When I've presented seitan recipes in my cooking classes, students have agreed that this wheat meat tastes a lot like beef, especially if it's flavored like a traditional beef dish—in this case a curry dish popular in the tropics. Premade seitan is available in various flavors and forms. For this recipe, choose a variety with a fairly neutral flavor.

tropical SEITAN CURRY

1 cup **water,** plus more as needed

1 small **yellow onion**

4 cups chopped fresh or no-salt-added **canned tomatoes** with liquid

1 pound **seitan,** cut into bite-sized pieces

1 cup no-salt-added **tomato sauce**

1 tablespoon **curry powder**

1/2 cup canned **pineapple chunks** packed in juice, liquid reserved

1 tablespoon **cornstarch**

1/2 cup chopped unsalted roasted **peanuts**

1 **banana,** thinly sliced (optional)

Unsweetened shredded **dried coconut** (optional)

Put 1/4 cup of the water in a large skillet, then add the onion. Cook over medium heat, stirring occasionally and adding more water as needed to prevent sticking, until the onion is translucent, about 10 minutes. Stir in the remaining water and the tomatoes, seitan, tomato sauce, and curry powder.

Drain the pineapple well, reserving 1/4 cup of the juice. Stir the cornstarch into the juice, then pour the mixture into the skillet. Decrease the heat to low and cook, stirring occasionally, until the sauce has thickened quite a bit, about 30 minutes.

Just before serving, add the pineapple and peanuts and cook, stirring occasionally, until heated through, about 3 minutes. Serve topped with the optional banana and sprinkled with coconut if desired.

Per serving: 315 calories, 27 g protein, 12 g fat (1 g sat), 31 g carbs, 34 mg sodium, 44 mg calcium, 6 g fiber

I recommend that, rather than assembling individual tacos, you put all the fixin's out on the table in small bowls. That way everyone can make their own tacos with just the ingredients they prefer. It's far less likely that mealtime will become a battleground if everybody feels like they're making their own decisions about what to eat.

overstuffed SOFT TACOS

See photo facing page 53.

MAKES 4 SERVINGS

8 (6-inch) **corn tortillas,** briefly warmed in a toaster oven or microwave

1 cup vegan **refried beans,** warmed

1 ripe **avocado,** sliced and sprinkled lightly with lemon juice (to prevent browning)

1 ripe **mango,** cut into small pieces (see tip, page 47)

$1/2$ cup shredded **romaine lettuce,** lightly packed

$1/2$ cup **baby salad greens,** lightly packed

$1/2$ cup **baby spinach,** lightly packed

$1/2$ cup chopped **red bell pepper**

2 **green onions,** thinly sliced

$1/4$ cup finely chopped **red onion**

$1/4$ cup **alfalfa sprouts**

$1/4$ cup pitted **olives,** chopped

$1/4$ cup **salsa**

$1/4$ cup chopped **cilantro** (optional)

Put all the ingredients in individual bowls and allow everyone to assemble their own tacos as desired.

Per serving: 381 calories, 12 g protein, 29 g fat (1 g sat), 61 g carbs, 492 mg sodium, 89 mg calcium, 15 g fiber

This satisfying chili is a meal in a bowl. Plus, it keeps well, so any leftovers will be at the ready when hunger strikes and time for meal prep is short.

chili SIN CARNE

¼ cup **water,** plus more as needed

2 **onions,** chopped

2 **carrots,** shredded

1 **zucchini,** quartered lengthwise and sliced ½ inch thick

1 **green bell pepper,** chopped

1 cup raw **cashews,** chopped

2 cloves **garlic,** finely chopped

4 cups chopped fresh or no-salt-added **canned tomatoes** with liquid

2 cans (15 ounces each) no-salt-added **kidney beans,** drained and rinsed

1 can (6 ounces) no-salt-added **tomato paste**

2 tablespoons **chili powder**

1 teaspoon dried **basil**

1 teaspoon ground **cumin**

1 teaspoon dried **oregano**

1 teaspoon **paprika**

Pinch **cayenne**

1 **bay leaf**

4 ounces **vegan burger crumbles,** thawed if frozen

2 cups cooked **brown rice** or **quinoa** (see page 11)

Put the water in a large pot, then add the onions, carrots, zucchini, bell pepper, cashews, and garlic. Cook over medium heat, stirring occasionally and adding more water as needed to prevent sticking, until the onions are translucent, about 10 minutes.

Stir in the tomatoes, beans, tomato paste, chili powder, basil, cumin, oregano, paprika, cayenne, and bay leaf. Decrease the heat to medium-low, cover, and cook, stirring occasionally, until the vegetables are very tender and the flavors have blended, about 1 hour.

Stir in the vegan burger crumbles and rice and cook, stirring occasionally, until heated through, about 15 minutes.

CHILI CON CORNY: Add 2 cups of fresh or frozen corn kernels when you add the beans.

Per serving: 598 calories, 32 g protein, 15 g fat (2 g sat), 89 g carbs, 274 mg sodium, 253 mg calcium, 30 g fiber

If members of your mixed household crave overstuffed restaurant burritos, this recipe will come to your rescue. Arugula can vary in flavor. Younger, baby varieties tend to be less spicy and bitter, so choose according to your family's palates.

BURSTING **burritos**

BEAN SPREAD

1 can (15 ounces) no-salt-added **Great Northern or cannellini beans,** drained and rinsed

1 **green onion,** trimmed (optional)

2 tablespoons **tahini**

2 tablespoons freshly squeezed **lemon juice**

1 clove **garlic,** finely chopped

½ teaspoon ground **cumin**

½ teaspoon **paprika**

Pinch **cayenne** (optional)

Salt

Ground **pepper**

To make the bean spread, put the beans, optional green onion, tahini, lemon juice, garlic, cumin, paprika, and optional cayenne in a food processor and process until smooth. Season with salt and pepper to taste.

To make the filling, put the water in a large skillet, then add the bell pepper and mushrooms. Cook over medium heat, stirring occasionally, until tender, about 10 minutes. Add the spinach and cook, stirring frequently, just until wilted, about 1 minute. Remove from the heat.

Put the tortillas on a work surface. Spread the beans over the tortillas, leaving a 1-inch border all the way around. Spread the cooked vegetables evenly over the beans. Top with the arugula. Arrange the tomatoes, cut-side down, in a line across the center. Spread the salsa in a thin layer over the fillings.

Fold in the sides, then roll up tightly from the bottom. Cut in half crosswise before serving.

Per serving: 387 calories, 15 g protein, 10 g fat (2 g sat), 60 g carbs, 802 mg sodium, 253 mg calcium, 15 g fiber

Note: Analysis doesn't include salt to taste.

FILLING AND WRAPPERS

1 tablespoon **water**

½ **red bell pepper,** chopped

4 ounces **mushrooms**

10 ounces **baby spinach**

4 large whole-grain **flour tortillas**

4 ounces **baby arugula**

1 cup **cherry tomatoes,** halved

½ cup **salsa**

TIPS

- If you're not wild about the taste of arugula, swap it out for an equal amount of baby salad greens.
- If you don't want to heat up the kitchen, or if you simply have a hankering for the crunch of raw vegetables, it's not necessary to cook the bell pepper, mushrooms, and spinach. Just decrease the spinach to 2 to 4 ounces and coarsely chop it.

These fajitas have plenty of pizzazz without being greasy, as restaurant versions so often are. Plus, this easy recipe has plenty of wiggle room to satisfy all palates at the dinner table. Depending on others' preferences, you may want to replace

FLEXIBLE **fajitas**

Juice of 1 **lime**

1 tablespoon **olive oil**

1 tablespoon **hoisin sauce**

½ **jalapeño chile,** seeded and finely chopped

2 cloves **garlic,** finely chopped

½ teaspoon ground **cumin**

¼ teaspoon **chili powder**

Pinch **cayenne** (optional)

¼ cup chopped fresh **cilantro,** lightly packed

8 ounces **tempeh,** halved crosswise, then sliced lengthwise into thin strips

1 tablespoon **vegetable oil**

1 sweet **yellow onion,** cut into thin half-moons

1 **green bell pepper,** cut into thin strips

1 **red bell pepper,** cut into thin strips

4 ounces **mushrooms,** thinly sliced

1 small **zucchini,** halved crosswise, then sliced lengthwise into thick strips

Put the lime juice, olive oil, hoisin sauce, chile, garlic, cumin, chili powder, and optional cayenne in a shallow bowl and stir with a fork until well blended. Stir in the cilantro. Add the tempeh and stir gently until evenly coated. Cover and let sit for 30 minutes, stirring occasionally.

Heat a large skillet, preferably cast-iron, over medium heat. Add the vegetable oil and swirl the pan until evenly coated with the oil. Add the tempeh (reserve the marinade) and cook, stirring occasionally, until lightly browned, 10 to 15 minutes.

Add the onion, green bell pepper, red bell pepper, mushrooms, and zucchini. Cook, stirring occasionally and adding the reserved marinade as needed to prevent sticking, just until tender, about 5 minutes.

Quiche Your Troubles Good-Bye, *page 92*

No-Beef Bourguignon, *page 98*

the tempeh with other plant-based proteins, such as vegan chicken strips, vegan beef tips, vegan prawns, or a combination. Load up the table with bowls of popular toppings so everyone can customize their fajitas to suit their tastes.

4 whole-grain **flour tortillas,** or 8 **corn tortillas**

Favorite fajita toppings, such as:

shredded romaine lettuce

chopped tomatoes

guacamole

vegan sour cream

shredded vegan cheese

fresh cilantro

and salsa (optional)

Briefly warm the tortillas in a toaster oven or microwave. Distribute the vegetables and tempeh among the tortillas. Add the optional fajita toppings of your choice. Roll or fold the tortillas to enclose the filling and toppings.

Per serving: 363 calories, 14 g protein, 15 g fat (3 g sat), 46 g carbs, 571 mg sodium, 127 mg calcium, 9 g fiber

TIPS FROM THE TRENCHES

"No arguments are necessary. I just let the food speak for itself. Now my partner says, 'You know, I feel a lot better when I skip the meat!' And of course, I'm delighted for both of us!"

This recipe features a bounty of delicious and colorful vegetables, with multicolored bow-tie pasta giving it even more eye appeal. The dish is also a great starting point for the addition of plant-based proteins. And it's a snap to prep the vegetables if you use the slicing disc of a food processor.

pasta PRIMAVERA

MAKES 6 SERVINGS

1 pound multicolored **bow-tie pasta**

¼ cup **water** or no-salt-added **vegetable broth,** plus more as needed

1 **sweet yellow onion,** thinly sliced

1 **carrot,** thinly sliced

4 cloves **garlic,** chopped

1 cup **broccoli florets**

1 cup **cauliflower florets**

8 ounces **button mushrooms,** thinly sliced

6 ounces **sugar snap peas,** trimmed and halved crosswise

2 cups shredded **red cabbage**

1 **yellow summer squash,** thinly sliced

1 **zucchini,** thinly sliced

1 **red bell pepper,** thinly sliced

1 **yellow bell pepper,** thinly sliced

2 **green onions,** thinly sliced

¼ cup pitted **black olives,** sliced

20 fresh **basil leaves,** thinly sliced

1 cup shredded vegan **mozzarella cheese**

Bring a large pot of water to a boil over high heat. Stir in the pasta. Decrease the heat to medium-low, cover, and cook, stirring occasionally, until tender but firm. Drain well.

Put the water in a large skillet, then add the yellow onion, carrot, and garlic. Cook over medium heat, stirring occasionally and adding more water as needed to prevent sticking, until the onion is translucent, about 10 minutes.

Add the broccoli and cauliflower and cook, stirring occasionally, for about 3 minutes. Add the mushrooms, sugar snap peas, cabbage, yellow squash, zucchini, bell peppers, and green onions and cook, stirring occasionally and adding more water as needed to prevent sticking, just until all the vegetables are tender, about 5 minutes.

Put the pasta in a large serving bowl. Add the cooked vegetables and olives and toss gently to combine. Scatter the basil on top, then sprinkle with the vegan cheese.

Per serving: 436 calories, 14 g protein, 6 g fat (1 g sat), 82 g carbs, 220 mg sodium, 120 mg calcium, 9 g fiber

Note: Analyzed with Daiya mozzarella-style shreds.

You may be surprised to learn that cheese and other dairy products contain compounds (called casomorphins) that have an opioid effect. Perhaps that explains why many people find that cheese is the hardest food to give up when switching to a vegan diet. With this recipe, everyone can have their pizza and eat it too, thanks to the bounty of vegan cheeses now available. Pick and choose your toppings. These are not set in stone.

GARDEN pizza

¼ cup **water**

1 cup thinly sliced **leek** (white part only)

1 cup shredded **carrots**

1 clove **garlic,** chopped

1 (12-inch) whole-grain **pizza crust**

1 cup shredded vegan **mozzarella cheese**

4 ripe **Roma tomatoes,** thinly sliced

½ **zucchini,** thinly sliced

½ green or red **bell pepper,** chopped

1 cup sliced thin **asparagus,** in ½-inch pieces

¼ cup pitted **olives,** sliced

1 teaspoon **Italian seasoning**

½ cup chopped fresh **basil,** lightly packed (optional)

Preheat the oven to 425 degrees F. Mist a 12-inch pizza pan with cooking spray.

Put the water in a medium skillet, then add the leek, carrots, and garlic. Cook over medium heat, stirring occasionally, until the leek is tender, about 5 minutes. Remove from the heat.

Put the crust on the prepared pan. Spread the vegan cheese evenly over the crust. Arrange the tomatoes evenly over the cheese. Spread the cooked leek mixture over the tomatoes. Top with the zucchini, bell pepper, asparagus, and olives, then sprinkle with the Italian seasoning.

Bake for about 15 minutes, until the crust is golden and the cheese has melted. Sprinkle the optional basil over the top and serve immediately.

Per serving: 435 calories, 14 g protein, 10 g fat (2 g sat), 79 g carbs, 752 mg sodium, 105 mg calcium, 13 g fiber

Note: Analyzed with Daiya mozzarella-style shreds.

Quinoa, a staple of the ancient Aztecs, has stood the test of time, and for good reason. It has more protein than wheat, rice, barley, and other grains, and it also boasts a delicious flavor and appealing crunchy texture. This is a great recipe for introducing skeptics to the joys of vegan eating.

QUINOA **paella**

2¼ cups **water**

1 **carrot,** finely chopped

1 **red bell pepper,** finely chopped

½ cup finely **chopped onion**

1 clove **garlic,** finely chopped

1 cup **quinoa**

¼ teaspoon ground **pepper**

¼ teaspoon ground **turmeric** or crushed **saffron threads**

4 ounces **vegan chicken,** thawed if frozen, cut into ½-inch cubes

4 ounces **vegan kielbasa** or **vegan turkey,** thawed if frozen, cut into ½-inch rounds or chunks

4 ounces **vegan prawns or shrimp,** thawed if frozen

1 cup frozen **petite peas**

4 **lemon wedges**

Put ¼ cup of the water in a large skillet, then add the carrot, bell pepper, onion, and garlic. Cook over medium heat, stirring occasionally and adding more water as needed to prevent sticking, just until the vegetables are tender, about 15 minutes.

Stir in the remaining water and the quinoa, pepper, and turmeric and bring to a boil over high heat. Decrease the heat to low, cover, and cook for 10 minutes.

Stir in the vegan chicken, vegan kielbasa, vegan prawns, and peas. Cover and cook until the quinoa is tender and everything is heated through, about 10 minutes. Serve garnished with the lemon wedges.

Per serving: 356 calories, 21 g protein, 8 g fat (0.4 g sat), 50 g carbs, 433 mg sodium, 126 mg calcium, 12 g fiber

TIP: If you'd like to substitute brown rice for the quinoa, simply increase the cooking time from 10 minutes to 40 minutes after stirring in the rice and bringing to a boil.

Let your taste buds sail away with this delectable and elegant main dish.

zucchini BOATS WITH KALE AND WHITE BEAN FILLING

$\frac{1}{2}$ cup no-salt-added **vegetable broth**

2 cups stemmed and chopped **kale,** lightly packed

8 ounces thin **asparagus,** cut into $\frac{1}{2}$-inch pieces

4 ounces **mushrooms,** chopped

2 **green onions,** cut into $\frac{1}{4}$-inch pieces

2 cloves **garlic,** chopped

2 tablespoons chopped fresh **dill,** or 2 teaspoons dried dill weed

1 can (15 ounces) no-salt-added **white beans,** drained and rinsed

1 tablespoon reduced-sodium **soy sauce**

1 teaspoon **balsamic vinegar**

$\frac{1}{4}$ teaspoon vegan **red chili paste**

4 large **zucchini**

1 cup shredded vegan **mozzarella cheese**

Preheat the oven to 350 degrees F. Line a rimmed baking sheet with parchment paper or mist it with cooking spray.

Put the broth in a medium skillet, then add the kale, asparagus, mushrooms, green onions, garlic, and dill. Cook over medium heat, stirring occasionally, until the vegetables are tender, about 10 minutes.

Put the beans, soy sauce, vinegar, and chili paste in a large bowl and mash until mostly smooth.

Cut the zucchini in half lengthwise and scoop out the flesh from the center, leaving enough that the zucchini boats hold their shape. Chop the zucchini flesh and add it to the bean mixture. Add the cooked vegetables and vegan cheese and stir to combine.

Put the zucchini boats on the lined baking sheet and fill them with the bean mixture. Bake for 25 to 30 minutes, until the zucchini boats are fork-tender.

Per serving: 276 calories, 14 g protein, 8 g fat (2 g sat), 41 g carbs, 562 mg sodium, 171 mg calcium, 11 g fiber

Note: Analyzed with Daiya mozzarella-style shreds.

These stuffed tomatoes are elegant enough to serve to even the most discerning diners.

tomatoes STUFFED WITH ALMOND PÂTÉ

MAKES 4 SERVINGS

4 large ripe **tomatoes**

1 large **sweet yellow onion,** coarsely chopped

½ cup raw or unsalted roasted **almonds**

½ cup **pine nuts**

1 package (10 ounces) frozen chopped **spinach,** thawed and all excess moisture pressed out

½ cup shredded vegan **mozzarella cheese** (optional)

Preheat the oven to 350 degrees F. Line an 11 x 8-inch baking pan with parchment paper or mist it with cooking spray.

Cut off the tops of the tomatoes. Scoop out the flesh from the center and put it in a food processor, leaving enough flesh that the tomatoes hold their shape and taking care to not puncture the skin. Put the tomatoes upside down on a plate to drain.

Add the onion, almonds, and pine nuts to the food processor and pulse until well combined and mostly smooth but some texture remains. Transfer to a medium bowl. Add the spinach and optional cheese and stir to combine.

Put the tomatoes right-side up in the lined pan. Spoon the spinach mixture into the hollows. Bake for about 20 minutes, until the filling is hot and steaming.

Per serving: 260 calories, 10 g protein, 17 g fat (2 g sat), 19 g carbs, 120 mg sodium, 136 mg calcium, 6 g fiber

It's five o'clock and you're clueless in the kitchen? No worries! This dish will have you covered.

FAST 'N' **fabulous** CABBAGE

½ cup **water,** plus more as needed

1 tablespoon **vegetable oil**

1 teaspoon low-sodium **vegetable broth powder**

1 package (10 ounces) **vegan chicken scallopini,** thawed if frozen, cut into bite-sized pieces

4 cups chopped **green cabbage,** in 2-inch pieces

2 ripe **tomatoes,** quartered

1 **green bell pepper,** chopped

½ cup chopped **yellow onion**

½ cup **raisins** or chopped **soft dates,** preferably medjool

2 tablespoons chopped fresh **parsley**

1 teaspoon **garlic powder**

1 teaspoon **onion powder**

1 teaspoon **paprika**

½ teaspoon ground **turmeric**

2 cups cooked **brown rice** or **millet** (see page 11)

1 cup shredded vegan **pepper Jack cheese**

Preheat the oven to 350 degrees F.

Put the water, oil, and broth powder in a large, ovenproof skillet and stir to combine. Add the vegan chicken, cabbage, tomatoes, bell pepper, onion, raisins, parsley, garlic powder, onion powder, paprika, and turmeric. Cook over medium heat, stirring occasionally and adding more water as needed to prevent sticking, just until the vegetables begin to soften, about 10 minutes. Stir in the rice.

Cover and cook on the stovetop over low heat or in the oven until the cabbage is tender, about 30 minutes. Sprinkle the vegan cheese over the top and bake for 5 to 10 minutes, until the cheese has melted and the cabbage is soft.

Per serving: 453 calories, 20 g protein, 15 g fat (3 g sat), 62 g carbs, 665 mg sodium, 110 mg calcium, 10 g fiber

Note: Analyzed with Daiya pepper Jack-style shreds.

Who says real men—or die-hard carnivores—don't eat quiche? This protein-packed version, with a tofu filling replete with colorful vegetables and embellished with vegan cheese, is bound to be popular with people of any dietary persuasion. This

quiche YOUR TROUBLES GOOD-BYE

See photo facing page 84.   MAKES 6 SERVINGS

CRUST

1 cup whole wheat **flour**

$1/2$ teaspoon **salt**

$1/4$ cup **olive oil**

$2^1/2$ tablespoons cold **water**

FILLING

$1/2$ **sweet yellow onion,** chopped

$1/4$ cup chopped **green bell pepper**

$1/4$ cup chopped **red bell pepper**

$1/4$ cup chopped **broccoli florets**

$1/4$ cup sliced **mushrooms**

$1/4$ cup coarsely chopped **spinach**

1 **green onion,** thinly sliced

2 cloves **garlic,** chopped

$1/2$ teaspoon dried **dill weed**

$1/2$ teaspoon dried **rosemary**

$1/4$ teaspoon dried **basil**

1 pound firm **silken tofu,** drained

$1/3$ cup shredded vegan **Cheddar cheese**

$1/3$ cup shredded vegan **mozzarella cheese**

$1/4$ teaspoon ground **turmeric**

Pinch ground **nutmeg**

Salt and ground **pepper**

To make the crust, put the flour and salt in a medium bowl and stir to combine. Add the oil and water and stir with a fork until the mixture comes together to form a dough. Form the dough into a ball and put it on a plate. Cover with a clean kitchen towel and let sit for 5 minutes.

Put the dough between two sheets of waxed paper and roll it out to a round about 12 inches in diameter. Transfer to a 9-inch pie pan. Press the dough into the pan and trim the edges or fold and press them to form a rim.

Preheat the oven to 350 degrees F.

To make the filling, mist a large skillet with cooking spray. Put the yellow onion, bell peppers, broccoli, mushrooms, spinach, green onion, and garlic in the skillet and cook over medium heat, stirring occasionally, just until the mushrooms begin to soften, about 5 minutes. Stir in the dill, rosemary, and basil and remove from the heat.

Put the tofu, $1/4$ cup of the vegan Cheddar, $1/4$ cup of the vegan mozzarella, and the turmeric and nutmeg in a food processor and process until uniformly golden in color and mostly smooth. Transfer to a medium bowl and stir in the cooked vegetables. Season with salt and pepper to taste. Pour the mixture into the crust and smooth the top with a rubber spatula.

recipe is very versatile. Feel free to switch up the vegetables or replace some of them with vegan meat analogs. For convenience, you can use a store-bought vegan crust or simply make a crustless quiche.

Bake for 40 minutes, until the crust is golden and a knife inserted in the center comes out clean. Sprinkle the remaining vegan cheese over the top, then bake for 5 to 10 minutes longer, until the cheese has melted. Let cool for 10 minutes before serving.

Per serving: 237 calories, 7 g protein, 14 g fat (2 g sat), 21 g carbs, 314 mg sodium, 48 mg calcium, 2 g fiber

Note: Analyzed with Daiya Cheddar-style and mozzarella-style shreds. Analysis doesn't include salt to taste.

INDIVIDUAL QUICHES: Mist six standard muffin cups with cooking spray or line them with silicone liners. Divide the dough into 6 equal portions and roll them out to rounds about 5 inches in diameter. Transfer to the prepared muffin cups, gently shaping the dough to fit the cups. Distribute the filling evenly among the muffin cups. Bake for about 25 minutes, until the crust is golden and a knife inserted in the center of a quiche comes out clean. Sprinkle the remaining vegan cheese over the quiches, then bake for 5 to 10 minutes longer, until the cheese has melted. Let cool for 10 minutes before serving.

When my kids were younger, they liked to go through my cookbooks, looking at the pictures and picking out the dishes they wanted to try. Using strategies like this, where others get to choose the menu, is huge in getting a buy-in at the

MUSHROOMS AND LENTILS IN **phyllo**

MAKES 6 SERVINGS

5 cups no-salt-added **vegetable broth**

2 **onions,** cut into half-moons

1¼ cups **long-grain brown rice**

Salt

Ground **pepper**

1 cup dried **green lentils,** soaked for 30 minutes

2 **bay leaves**

¼ cup **olive oil**

¼ cup **water**

2 tablespoons **Ener-G egg replacer**

¼ cup chopped fresh **parsley,** lightly packed

2 tablespoons chopped fresh **dill,** or 2 teaspoons dried dill weed

8 ounces **mushrooms,** sliced

8 sheets vegan **phyllo pastry** (see tip)

Put ¼ cup of the broth in a medium saucepan, then add half of the onions. Cook over medium heat, stirring occasionally, for 5 minutes.

Stir in the rice, then stir in 2¼ cups of the remaining broth. Decrease the heat to low, cover, and cook for about 45 minutes, until all the liquid is absorbed and the rice is tender. Remove from the heat and let sit covered for 5 minutes. Season with salt and pepper to taste.

Meanwhile, drain the lentils and put them in a medium saucepan with the remaining 2½ cups of broth, the remaining onion, and the bay leaves. Bring to a boil over high heat. Decrease the heat to medium-low, cover, and cook, stirring occasionally, until the lentils are tender, about 25 minutes. Drain well, then season with salt and pepper to taste.

Preheat the oven to 375 degrees F. Brush a 13 x 9-inch baking pan with a bit of the oil.

Put the water and egg replacer in a small bowl and stir until well combined. Add the mixture to the rice, along with the parsley and dill, and toss with two forks to combine.

Put 1 teaspoon of the oil in a small skillet over medium heat. Add the mushrooms and cook, stirring occasionally, just until they begin to soften, about 5 minutes. Season with salt and pepper to taste.

Lay 1 sheet of phyllo in the prepared pan, with half of it covering the base and the other half hanging equally over the long sides of the pan. Brush the phyllo within the pan generously with some of the oil. Continue in this way until all

table. Here's a Russian dish one of my daughters selected that soon became a weekly favorite, veganized here for your dining pleasure.

the phyllo has been layered in the pan, with the overhanging phyllo stacked but not oiled.

Spread half of the rice over the phyllo, top with half of the lentils, then top with half of the mushrooms. Repeat the layers using the remaining rice, lentils, and mushrooms. Fold the overhanging part of the phyllo sheets over the filling, one sheet at a time, covering the filling as fully as possible and brushing each with some of the oil before folding the next.

Bake for about 45 minutes, until the phyllo is golden and crisp. Let cool for 10 minutes before slicing and serving.

Per serving: 352 calories, 13 g protein, 2 g fat (0.3 g sat), 70 g carbs, 107 mg sodium, 9 mg calcium, 6 g fiber

Note: Analysis doesn't include salt to taste.

TIP: Don't feel intimidated about working with phyllo dough. The key is to thaw the phyllo in the refrigerator for a day or so before using it. The sheets will then be less likely to stick to each other, as they tend to do when phyllo is thawed more quickly. Don't stress if any of the pieces tear; the results will still be delicious. After you've worked with phyllo dough a time or two, you'll be much more confident.

The combination of chicken and rice is a comfort-food classic—even for vegans, thanks to the many plant-based chicken alternatives now available. Look for vegan chicken tenders or another form of faux chicken that's breaded.

vegan CHICKEN AND RICE

2½ cups **water**

1 teaspoon low-sodium **vegetable broth powder**

8 ounces **mushrooms,** sliced

½ cup chopped **celery**

½ cup chopped **onion**

½ cup **raisins** (optional)

¼ cup chopped **green bell pepper**

1 cup **long-grain brown rice**

8 ounces frozen **vegan crispy chicken strips,** prepared according to the package instructions and kept hot

Put ½ cup of the water and the broth powder in a medium saucepan and stir to combine. Add the mushrooms, celery, onion, optional raisins, and bell pepper and cook over medium heat, stirring occasionally, for 5 minutes.

Stir in the rice, then stir in the remaining water. Bring to a boil over high heat. Decrease the heat to low, cover, and cook for about 45 minutes, until all the liquid is absorbed and the rice is tender. Serve the vegan chicken strips over the rice.

Per serving: 303 calories, 16 g protein, 6 g fat (1 g sat), 48 g carbs, 264 mg sodium, 62 mg calcium, 5 g fiber

TIPS FROM THE TRENCHES

"Be true to yourself and allow others to do the same."

Superfoods abound in this supremely satisfying entrée. The tomatoes are rich in lycopene and other antioxidants, the sweet potatoes are an amazing source of beta-carotene, and kale is simply one of the most healthful foods you can eat, hands down.

SWEET POTATO AND KALE casserole

2 cans (28 ounces each) no-salt-added chopped **tomatoes**

1 can (6 ounces) no-salt-added **tomato paste**

1 can (5.5 ounces) **coconut milk**

3 cloves **garlic,** finely chopped

1 teaspoon vegan **red chili paste**

4 **sweet potatoes,** peeled and cut into ¼-inch-thick rounds

4 cups stemmed and chopped **kale,** steamed until tender

2 cups chopped **vegan turkey** (optional)

1 cup shredded **vegan cheese** (Cheddar, mozzarella, or a combination)

Preheat the oven to 350 degrees F.

Put the tomatoes, tomato paste, coconut milk, garlic, and chili paste in a medium bowl and stir until the tomato paste is evenly distributed.

Spread one-third of the mixture in a 13 x 9-inch baking pan. Arrange half of the sweet potatoes evenly over the top. Top with half of the kale, followed by half of the vegan turkey. Repeat the layers, beginning with another one-third of the tomato mixture and topping with the remaining sweet potatoes, kale, and optional turkey. Spread the remaining tomato mixture evenly over the top.

Bake for about 30 minutes, until the sweet potatoes are fork-tender. Sprinkle the vegan cheese over the top, then bake for 5 to 10 minutes longer, until the cheese has melted.

Per serving: 436 calories, 11 g protein, 14 g fat (8 g sat), 66 g carbs, 407 mg sodium, 412 mg calcium, 12 g fiber

Note: Analyzed with Daiya mozzarella-style shreds.

I highly recommend that you use porcini mushrooms in this recipe. They are less expensive than most other varieties of dried mushrooms but have a rich flavor and create a lush gravy.

NO-BEEF **bourguignon**

See photo facing page 85.

See photo facing page 85.

MAKES 4 SERVINGS

1½ ounces dried **mushrooms,** preferably porcini (see tip)

1 **yellow onion,** chopped

2 cloves **garlic,** finely chopped

1½ cups **water**

6 **new red potatoes,** scrubbed and quartered

¾ cup **Burgundy wine** or **red grape juice**

2 tablespoons no-salt-added **tomato paste**

1 teaspoon dried **thyme**

1 **bay leaf**

8 ounces frozen **pearl onions**

8 ounces fresh **green beans,** trimmed and halved crosswise, or frozen cut green beans

8 ounces vegan **beef tips,** thawed if frozen

6 strips vegan **bacon,** diced

TIP: You can substitute fresh mushrooms for the dried mushrooms. Use 8 ounces of fresh mushrooms, sliced, and add them along with the yellow onion. (Fresh mushrooms shouldn't be soaked.)

Put the mushrooms in a bowl and add boiling water to cover generously. Put a plate or smaller bowl on top of the mushrooms to keep them submerged. Let sit until tender; the time will vary depending on the mushrooms, but about 20 minutes should suffice for most varieties. Drain well. You might want to save the flavorful mushroom soaking water to use in place of the water in this recipe; if you do, strain it through a coffee filter to remove any grit. If the mushrooms are whole, slice them.

Mist a large nonstick skillet with cooking spray, then add the mushrooms, yellow onion, and garlic. Cook over medium heat, stirring occasionally, until the onion is translucent, about 10 minutes.

Stir in the water (or the strained mushroom soaking liquid plus water as needed to equal 1½ cups) and the potatoes, wine, tomato paste, thyme, and bay leaf. Bring to a boil over high heat. Decrease the heat to low, cover, and cook, stirring occasionally, until the potatoes are almost tender, 15 to 20 minutes. Stir in the pearl onions and green beans and cook, stirring occasionally, until tender, about 10 minutes.

While the green beans are cooking, mist a medium skillet with cooking spray, then add the vegan beef tips and vegan bacon. Cook over medium heat, stirring frequently, until lightly browned, 5 to 10 minutes. Add to the potato mixture and stir until evenly distributed.

Per serving: 361 calories, 18 g protein, 4 g fat (0.3 g sat), 42 g carbs, 454 mg sodium, 69 mg calcium, 9 g fiber

Thanks to the delectable grill flavors, these kabobs will please people of any dietary persuasion. If any of the veggies called for are less than beloved by your beloved, simply leave them out—or try substituting other vegetables with a higher approval rating. You can serve the kabobs atop any cooked whole grain, presenting yet another opportunity to fine-tune the meal based on diners' preferences.

COLORFUL **kabobs**

MAKES 4 SERVINGS

MARINATED VEGAN DOGS

¼ cup **red wine vinegar**

2 tablespoons **olive oil**

1 tablespoon reduced-sodium **soy sauce**

1 small clove **garlic,** chopped

½ teaspoon dried **parsley**

½ teaspoon dried **rosemary**

½ teaspoon dried **thyme**

4 large **vegan hot dogs,** each cut crosswise on the diagonal into 4 equal pieces

VEGETABLES

16 **cherry tomatoes**

1 **green bell pepper,** cut into 16 squares

1 **red or yellow bell pepper,** cut into 16 squares

1 **zucchini,** cut into 16 thick half-moons

1 **yellow summer squash,** cut into 16 thick half-moons

16 cremini or button **mushrooms**

16 frozen **pearl onions,** thawed

To marinate the vegan hot dogs, put the vinegar, oil, soy sauce, garlic, parsley, rosemary, and thyme in a medium bowl and whisk until well blended. Pierce the vegan hot dog pieces with a fork once or twice to help them absorb the marinade. Put them in the bowl with the marinade and toss until evenly coated. Cover and refrigerate for at least 1 hour or up to 24 hours, stirring occasionally. Drain, reserving the excess marinade.

To assemble and cook the kabobs, preheat a grill or grill pan to medium-high heat.

Thread a cherry tomato, green bell pepper square, red bell pepper square, zucchini half-moon, yellow squash half-moon, mushroom, onion, and piece of vegan hot dog onto a skewer in that order, then repeat one more time per skewer. Fill the remaining seven skewers in the same way.

Put the skewers on the grill and cook, rotating as needed and basting with the reserved marinade, until the edges of the vegetables begin to brown, about 20 minutes.

Per serving: 224 calories, 20 g protein, 8 g fat (1 g sat), 22 g carbs, 843 mg sodium, 101 mg calcium, 3 g fiber

TIP: You'll need eight metal skewers for this recipe.

chapter eight

AGREEABLE APPETIZERS AND SIMPATICO SIDES

Appetizers and side dishes can do a great deal to bridge a kitchen divide. As enticing precursors or interludes, they set the stage for the tasty dishes to follow. If you're in the difficult position of having to cook different meals for other family members, the recipes in this chapter will serve you well. Many of them are nutritious enough that you and any other vegans in the household could make a meal of just the side dishes. Mix and match them to your heart's content, or serve them before or alongside any of the salads, soups, and main dishes in this book. It's easy to craft original and exciting meals this way. Of course, the "little bites" in this chapter make great party fare too.

For a change of pace from guacamole, try this sophisticated avocado dip. It's delicious on crostini, crackers, or crudités, especially bell peppers or tender young asparagus spears.

avocado DIP

1 ripe **avocado**

2 tablespoons chopped fresh flat-leaf **parsley** or **cilantro**

1 tablespoon **tarragon vinegar** or **rice vinegar**

1 clove **garlic,** chopped

½ teaspoon dried **tarragon**

½ teaspoon **capers**

Cut the avocado in half. Remove the pit and scoop the flesh into a food processor. Add the parsley, vinegar, garlic, tarragon, and capers and process until smooth. Serve immediately, or cover with plastic wrap pressed against the surface of the dip to prevent browning and refrigerate for up to 6 hours.

Per serving: 82 calories, 1 g protein, 7 g fat (1 g sat), 5 g carbs, 13 mg sodium, 12 mg calcium, 4 g fiber

TIPS FROM THE TRENCHES

"I'm the lone vegan in a house full of meat eaters, but I'm married to a wonderful man who cooks vegan meals for me and makes sure we eat out at places that have vegan options."

Move over bean dip! This edamame-based version is packed with protein and the zippy flavor of Dijon mustard. Try it on unconventional crudités, such as sugar snap peas, snow peas, or jicama spears. It's also a great spread for whole-grain crackers.

MUSTARDY **edamame** DIP

MAKES 4 SERVINGS

1½ cups shelled fresh (see tip, page 55) or frozen **edamame**

¼ cup **Dijon mustard**

1 clove **garlic,** chopped

1 teaspoon finely chopped **hot chile**

Bring a medium pot of water to a boil over high heat. Add the edamame. Return to a boil, decrease the heat to medium, and cook until tender, about 5 minutes. Drain, then rinse with cold water. (If the edamame you're using is precooked, there is no need to boil it, so this entire step may be skipped.)

Put the edamame, mustard, garlic, and chile in a food processor and process until smooth. Stored in a covered container in the refrigerator, the dip will keep for 5 days.

Per serving: 132 calories, 10 g protein, 7 g fat (2 g sat), 7 g carbs, 326 mg sodium, 46 mg calcium, 6 g fiber

A cousin to raw vegetable platters, this appetizer varies in that most of the vegetables are lightly steamed, yet they are still quite suitable for dipping in the tempting cashew-based aïoli.

VEGETABLE **platter** WITH CASHEW AÏOLI

CASHEW AÏOLI

¼ cup shelled fresh (see tip, page 55) or frozen **edamame**

1 cup raw **cashews**

¼ cup balsamic **vinegar,** preferably pear-infused

Juice of 1 **lemon**

4 cloves **garlic,** chopped

1 teaspoon **Dijon mustard**

VEGETABLES

6 small **artichokes,** trimmed

4 ounces small **red potatoes,** scrubbed and halved or quartered, depending on size

½ head **cauliflower,** cut into florets

4 **carrots,** sliced ¼ inch thick on the diagonal

4 ounces fresh **green beans,** trimmed

4 ounces **snow peas,** trimmed

1 small **zucchini,** cut into ¼-inch-thick rounds

1 **red bell pepper,** cut into thin strips

1 **yellow bell pepper,** cut into thin strips

1 cup **cherry tomatoes**

To make the aïoli, bring a small pot of water to a boil. Add the edamame. Return to a boil, decrease the heat to medium, and cook until tender, about 5 minutes. Drain, then rinse with cold water.

Transfer to a food processor. Add the cashews, vinegar, lemon juice, garlic, and mustard and process until smooth.

To prepare the vegetables, put the artichokes and potatoes in a large pot and add water to cover generously. Bring to a boil over high heat. Decrease the heat to low, cover, and cook until the potatoes are tender, about 20 minutes.

Using a slotted spoon, transfer the potatoes to a colander (let the artichokes continue to cook). Drain the potatoes well, then transfer to a serving platter. Cook the artichokes until tender (a fork inserted in the bottom of the stem end should slide in easily), about 20 minutes longer. Drain well and let the artichokes cool.

Meanwhile, put about ½ inch of water in a large skillet with a tight-fitting lid, then add the cauliflower and carrots. Bring to a boil over high heat. Decrease the heat to medium-low, cover, and cook just until beginning to soften but still crunchy, about 5 minutes. Using a slotted spoon, transfer to the colander and drain well. Transfer to the serving platter.

Put the green beans, snow peas, zucchini, and bell peppers in the skillet. Bring to a boil over high heat, then decrease the heat to low, cover, and cook just until beginning to soften but still crunchy, 2 to 3 minutes. Drain well in the colander, then transfer to the serving platter. Top with the cherry tomatoes.

When the artichokes are cool enough to handle, gently spread the leaves apart, exposing the fuzzy choke. Using a small spoon, preferably a serrated grapefruit spoon, scoop out and discard the choke.

To serve, put the artichokes on individual plates. Spoon the sauce into the cavities of the artichokes or put the sauce in a bowl. Serve the vegetable platter separately so everyone can take the vegetables of their choice.

Per serving: 262 calories, 11 g protein, 9 g fat (2 g sat), 40 g carbs, 187 mg sodium, 124 mg calcium, 13 g fiber

TIPS FROM THE TRENCHES

"I make all-vegan meals and supply some animal-based staples for the rest of the family, such as mayo, eggs, cheese, milk, turkey bacon, sliced turkey, and chicken strips. They are welcome to add any of these items to their plates. This keeps mealtime positive and peaceful for everyone."

Rich, sophisticated, and supremely flavorful, this dip will wow guests at a dinner party. It also makes a great spread for sandwiches or wraps.

nuts-ABOUT-YOU DIP

1 cup pitted **kalamata olives,** plus more if desired

1 cup fresh **basil leaves,** lightly packed

¼ cup roasted **almond butter,** plus more if desired

Juice of 1 **lemon**

1 tablespoon **capers**

1 clove **garlic,** chopped

Put all the ingredients in a food processor and process until smooth. For a creamier consistency, add more olives or almond butter and process again. Stored in a covered container in the refrigerator, the dip will keep for 3 days.

Per serving: 100 calories, 2 g protein, 8 g fat (1 g sat), 4 g carbs, 260 mg sodium, 35 mg calcium, 1 g fiber

TIPS FROM THE TRENCHES

"I cook a vegan dinner at home, and if my partner wants to cook meat, he can. When we eat out, it's no holds barred. Everyone eats and orders what they want."

I recommend that you keep a container of hummus in the refrigerator at all times. It's a good standby for those inevitable times when hunger pangs hit but a meal is no-where in sight. In addition to being great stuffed in pita bread, scooped atop lettuce leaves, or served as a dip with crudités, hummus can be thinned with vinegar to make an impromptu high-protein salad dressing.

NO-FRILLS **hummus**

2 cans (15 ounces each) no-salt-added **garbanzo beans,** drained and rinsed

¼ cup **water,** plus more if needed

¼ cup freshly squeezed **lemon juice**

2 tablespoons **tahini**

2 cloves **garlic**

1 teaspoon ground **cumin**

¼ teaspoon **salt**

Put all the ingredients in a food processor or blender and process until smooth. If the mixture is too thick to process properly, add more water, 1 tablespoon at a time.

Per serving: 142 calories, 7 g protein, 3 g fat (0.3 g sat), 20 g carbs, 111 mg sodium, 62 mg calcium, 5 g fiber

TIPS

- If you're really in a hurry or want to reduce the fat content, you can substitute more water for the tahini.
- If you have time, jazz up the hummus by stirring in a sliced green onion, a chopped roasted red bell pepper, or both. Or, if you're feeling adventurous, try stirring in about ¼ cup of chopped fresh mango.

Like hummus, these crunchy, delicious beans are wonderful to make in advance so that you always have a quick, high-protein snack at the ready.

crispy GARBANZO BEANS

MAKES 4 SERVINGS

2 cans (15 ounces each) no-salt-added **garbanzo beans**

1 teaspoon **Cajun blackened seasoning mix** (see tip)

Salt

Preheat the oven to 400 degrees F. Mist a rimmed baking sheet with cooking spray.

Drain the beans, rinse them well, then pat dry with a clean kitchen towel. Remove any loose skins. Spread the beans on the prepared baking sheet, then roll them around to lightly coat with the cooking spray.

Bake for 15 minutes. Remove from the oven, sprinkle with the seasoning mix, then season with salt. Roll the beans around again to evenly coat them with the seasoning. Bake for 5 minutes, then roll the beans around one more time. Bake for about 5 minutes longer, until golden and crisp.

Per serving: 229 calories, 12 g protein, 2 g fat (0 g sat), 37 g carbs, 118 mg sodium, 110 mg calcium, 9 g fiber

Note: Analysis doesn't include salt to taste.

TIP: I especially like the blend labeled "blackened redfish spice" for this recipe, but you can use any spice or spice blend you prefer. Strong-flavored seasonings—such as cayenne, ground cinnamon, curry powder, garlic powder, and onion powder—work especially well.

Elegant yet easy to put together, these stuffed mushrooms will be the life of the party.

STUFFED **mushrooms**

12 large **mushrooms**

¼ cup **water,** plus more as needed

1 teaspoon low-sodium **vegetable broth powder**

1 **onion,** finely chopped

4 cloves **garlic,** finely chopped

1 pound fresh **spinach,** chopped, or
    1 package (10 ounces) frozen chopped
    spinach, thawed and drained

1¼ cups shredded vegan **mozzarella cheese**

¼ cup finely chopped **walnuts**

2 tablespoons chopped fresh **dill,**
    or 2 teaspoons dried dill weed

Salt

Ground **pepper**

Preheat the oven to 350 degrees F. Line an 11 x 8-inch baking pan with parchment paper or mist it with cooking spray.

Remove the mushroom stems and chop them finely.

Put the water and broth powder in a small skillet and stir to combine, then add the onion and garlic. Cook over medium heat, stirring occasionally and adding more water as needed to prevent sticking, until the onion is translucent, about 10 minutes. Add the spinach and mushroom stems and cook, stirring often, just until the spinach is wilted, 3 to 5 minutes.

Remove from the heat and drain off any excess moisture. Add 1 cup of the vegan cheese and the walnuts and dill and stir until well combined. Season with salt and pepper to taste.

Put the mushrooms in the lined pan, placing them gill-side up. Distribute the filling among the mushrooms.

Bake for about 10 minutes, until the mushrooms are browned and juicy. Sprinkle the remaining ¼ cup of vegan cheese over the mushrooms, then bake for 5 to 10 minutes longer, until the cheese has melted.

Per serving: 150 calories, 5 g protein, 9 g fat (2 g sat), 15 g carbs, 302 mg sodium, 106 mg calcium, 4 g fiber
Note: Analyzed with Daiya mozzarella-style shreds. Analysis doesn't include salt to taste.

These cheesy pastries are a refined offering at parties. Although puff pastry and vegan cheese definitely don't earn the highest nutritional ratings, occasionally satisfying cravings for the distinctive flavors and textures of not-so-healthful foods can help anyone stick to a better diet overall. Even those who aren't fond of spinach won't be able to resist these.

SPINACH-CHEESE **straws**

MAKES 8 SERVINGS

1 package (10 ounces) frozen chopped **spinach,** thawed and all excess moisture pressed out

¾ cup shredded vegan **cheese** (Cheddar, pepper Jack, or a combination)

½ package (8.5 ounces) vegan **puff pastry,** thawed according to the package directions

Preheat the oven to 350 degrees F. Line a baking sheet with parchment paper.

Put the spinach and vegan cheese in a medium bowl and stir to combine.

Unfold the pastry sheet on a lightly floured work surface. Spread half of the spinach mixture evenly over the pastry. Roll lightly with a rolling pin, gently pushing the mixture into the dough. Fold the pastry in half, then gently roll it out to about its original dimensions.

Spread the remaining spinach mixture evenly over the pastry and roll lightly to press it into the dough. Cut the dough into strips about ½ inch wide. Twist each strip a couple of times. Arrange the strips on the lined baking sheet about 2 inches apart.

Bake for about 15 minutes, until puffed and golden brown.

Per serving: 144 calories, 3 g protein, 9 g fat (4 g sat), 13 g carbs, 194 mg sodium, 42 mg calcium, 2 g fiber

Note: Analyzed with Daiya Cheddar-style shreds.

In traditional versions of this dish, the slivered almonds seem like little more than a decorative garnish. Here, I've upped the quantity of almonds to capitalize on their protein, nutritional value, and crunchy appeal.

green bean ALMONDINE PLEASER

MAKES 4 SERVINGS

½ cup no-salt-added **vegetable broth**

12 ounces fresh **green beans,** trimmed

1 **red bell pepper,** chopped

4 cloves **garlic,** finely chopped

1 cup slivered or sliced **almonds**

¼ cup chopped fresh **parsley,** lightly packed

Put the broth in a large skillet, then add the green beans, bell pepper, and garlic. Cook over medium heat, stirring occasionally, until the vegetables are tender, 8 to 10 minutes. Remove from the heat and stir in the almonds and parsley.

Per serving: 209 calories, 8 g protein, 15 g fat (1 g sat), 15 g carbs, 8 mg sodium, 79 mg calcium, 8 g fiber

TIP: Feel free to substitute unsalted roasted cashews, unsalted roasted peanuts, or walnuts for the almonds.

There's no point in stewing over small things. But a recipe that warms people's hearts is no small thing, and this one will do the job nicely. For a filling meal, serve the stew over cooked whole grains.

ROOTIN' FOR YOU STEWED **vegetables**

1 cup no-salt-added **vegetable broth**

2 **yellow onions,** cut into thick half-moons

2 **carrots,** chopped

2 stalks **celery,** chopped

1 **leek** (white and tender green parts only), cut into ¼-inch-thick rounds

6 cloves **garlic,** finely chopped

8 large ripe **tomatoes,** chopped

6 **turnips,** scrubbed and cut into bite-sized pieces

6 **red potatoes,** scrubbed and cut into bite-sized pieces

6 leaves **Swiss chard,** stemmed and cut into thin strips

8 ounces **spinach** or **kale,** stemmed and cut into thin strips

1 **bay leaf**

Put the broth in a large pot, then add the onions, carrots, celery, leek, and garlic. Cook over medium heat, stirring occasionally, until the onions are translucent, about 10 minutes.

Stir in the tomatoes, turnips, potatoes, chard, spinach, and bay leaf. Decrease the heat to medium-low, cover, and cook, stirring occasionally, until all the vegetables are tender, about 20 minutes.

Per serving: 287 calories, 10 g protein, 1 g fat (0.2 g sat), 63 g carbs, 267 mg sodium, 164 mg calcium, 12 g fiber

Fresh asparagus needs only a light touch and minimal seasonings to capitalize on its delicate flavor. This effortless recipe helps you take ready advantage of asparagus when it's in season.

roasted ASPARAGUS

1 pound **asparagus,** trimmed

Juice of 1 **lemon**

2 tablespoons chopped fresh flat-leaf **parsley**

4 cloves **garlic,** finely chopped

Preheat the oven to 400 degrees F. Line a 13 x 9-inch baking pan with parchment paper or mist it with cooking spray.

Put the asparagus in the lined pan in a single layer. Cover with foil and bake for 10 minutes. Uncover and bake for about 10 minutes longer, until fork-tender.

Put the lemon juice, parsley, and garlic in a small bowl and stir to combine. Drizzle the mixture evenly over the asparagus and toss gently to coat.

Per serving: 32 calories, 3 g protein, 0 g fat (0 g sat), 7 g carbs, 6 mg sodium, 126 mg calcium, 3 g fiber

TIPS FROM THE TRENCHES

"Usually I make something that my partner can easily add meat to. Or I make two dishes—one for her and one for me. Quite often, though, she just appreciates that I cooked and is willing to have whatever I'm having."

Eggplant is so versatile, yet many cooks feel unsure about how to use it. If that sounds like you, this recipe, which is akin to eggplant Parmesan, will get you started. To transform the dish into a satisfying entrée, serve the eggplant on a bed of cooked brown rice.

HERBED eggplant SLICES

MAKES 4 SERVINGS

1 large **eggplant,** sliced lengthwise in ½-inch-thick slabs

2 large ripe **tomatoes,** chopped

4 cloves **garlic,** finely chopped

1 teaspoon dried **basil**

1 teaspoon dried **oregano**

1 teaspoon dried **parsley**

1 teaspoon dried **rosemary**

Salt

Ground **pepper**

1 cup grated vegan **Parmesan** or shredded vegan **mozzarella cheese**

Preheat the oven to 350 degrees F. Line a rimmed baking sheet with parchment paper or mist it with cooking spray.

Put the eggplant on the lined baking sheet in a single layer. Spread the tomatoes evenly over the eggplant. Sprinkle with the garlic, basil, oregano, parsley, and rosemary. Season with salt and pepper.

Bake for about 30 minutes, until the eggplant is very tender. Sprinkle the vegan cheese over the top, then bake for 5 to 10 minutes longer, until the cheese has melted.

Per serving: 146 calories, 15 g protein, 1 g fat (0.1 g sat), 19 g carbs, 339 mg sodium, 281 mg calcium, 12 g fiber

Note: Analyzed with Galaxy Nutritional Foods parmesan-flavored topping. Analysis doesn't include salt to taste.

While it's easy to cook vegetables on top of the stove, roasting them brings out a special sweetness and texture. In fact, they are so satisfying when prepared this way that minimal seasoning is needed. This recipe contains a wide variety of vegetables. They are left whole or cut into large pieces so that diners can select the items that appeal to them. Grab a knife and fork and dig in!

roasted VEGETABLES

2 **sweet yellow onions,** peeled and quartered

3 **zucchini,** quartered lengthwise

1 small **eggplant,** quartered lengthwise

8 ounces fresh **green beans,** trimmed

6 small **red potatoes,** scrubbed and halved

6 very small **beets,** trimmed

3 small **turnips,** trimmed and halved

3 **carrots,** scrubbed and halved lengthwise

Olive oil (optional)

Fresh or dried **herbs** (optional)

Salt

Pepper

Preheat the oven to 375 degrees F. Mist 2 large rimmed baking sheets with cooking spray.

Put the onions on one of the prepared baking sheets cut-side down. Add the zucchini and eggplant cut-side up. Add the green beans, placing them in any spaces between the other vegetables if need be. Put the potatoes, beets, turnips, and carrots on the other prepared baking sheet. Mist all the vegetables with additional cooking spray if desired.

Bake for about 30 minutes, until the onions, zucchini, eggplant, and green beans are fork-tender. Remove the baking sheet with the onions from the oven and cover loosely with foil to keep warm if desired. Continue baking the potatoes, beets, turnips, and carrots until fork-tender, 15 to 30 minutes longer. Sprinkle the vegetables with olive oil and herbs if desired. Season with salt and pepper to taste.

Per serving: 238 calories, 8 g protein, 1 g fat (0.1 g sat), 53 g carbs, 121 mg sodium, 89 mg calcium, 12 g fiber

Note: Analysis doesn't include salt to taste.

TIP: Any leftovers will be a fabulous addition to soups, salads, and other dishes.

These stuffed peppers are lighter than typical versions with grain-based fillings. Their sophisticated flavors make them great fare for a dinner party.

stuffed PEPPERS

2 **red bell peppers,** tops removed, seeded, and halved lengthwise

2 cups chopped **yellow onions**

1 cup pitted **olives,** chopped

1/2 cup shredded fresh **basil leaves,** lightly packed

2 cloves **garlic,** finely chopped

1/2 teaspoon **herbes de Provence**

1/2 cup shredded vegan **mozzarella cheese**

Preheat the oven to 350 degrees F. Line an 11 x 8-inch baking pan with parchment paper or mist it with cooking spray.

Arrange the pepper halves in the lined pan. Put the onions, olives, basil, garlic, and herbes de Provence in a medium bowl and stir to combine. Spoon the mixture into the pepper halves.

Bake for about 30 minutes, until the peppers are fork-tender and the onions are translucent. Sprinkle the vegan cheese over the peppers, then bake for 5 to 10 minutes longer, until the cheese has melted.

Per serving: 135 calories, 2 g protein, 3 g fat (1 g sat), 16 g carbs, 153 mg sodium, 35 mg calcium, 6 g fiber

Note: Analyzed with Daiya mozzarella-style shreds.

As-You-Like-It Risotto, *page 123*

Date Night Truffles, *page 135*

These potatoes could hardly be simpler to prepare, yet they're so elegant. As a bonus, you can bake the potatoes in the oven alongside another dish. If you do that, you may need to bake both dishes a few minutes longer than called for in their recipes.

DILLY **potatoes**

1½ pounds **small potatoes,** such as fingerling or new red, scrubbed

2 tablespoons chopped fresh **dill,** or 2 teaspoons dried dill weed

2 tablespoons chopped fresh **parsley,** or 2 teaspoons dried

1 tablespoon **olive oil** (optional)

Preheat the oven to 350 degrees F. Mist a heavy casserole dish with cooking spray.

Cut the potatoes in half, or quarter them if they are large. Put the potatoes in the prepared casserole dish. Sprinkle with the dill, parsley, and optional olive oil and stir until evenly distributed.

Cover and bake for about 1 hour, until the potatoes are fork-tender.

Per serving: 143 calories, 5 g protein, 0 g fat (0 g sat), 29 g carbs, 1 mg sodium, 23 mg calcium, 4 g fiber

TIP: If you love dill and parsley, feel free to double the amounts and save some in reserve to garnish the finished dish.

TIPS FROM THE TRENCHES

"We cook separately when we eat in. My partner is an absolute carnivore, but he goes to vegan restaurants with me and scarfs the food down heartily with no complaints."

This recipe takes classic latkes over the top by adding carrots for color and extra flavor.

POTATO **pancakes**

MAKES 6 SERVINGS

3 large starchy **potatoes,** such as russets, scrubbed and quartered

1 **onion,** peeled and quartered

1 **carrot,** trimmed

¼ cup unsweetened **nondairy milk**

1½ teaspoons **Ener-G egg replacer**

1 teaspoon **baking powder**

1 teaspoon **baking soda**

1 cup whole wheat or brown rice **flour**

2 tablespoons chopped fresh **parsley,** plus more for garnish

Preheat the oven to 300 degrees F. Have a nonstick baking sheet ready or line a baking sheet with parchment paper.

Put several inches of cold water in a large bowl. Grate the potatoes in a food processor or by hand. Transfer to the bowl of water to prevent browning. Grate the onion and carrot in the food processor.

Put the nondairy milk, egg replacer, baking powder, and baking soda in a large bowl and stir until well combined. Add the flour and parsley and stir vigorously until well combined.

Drain the potatoes well in a colander or fine-mesh strainer, then squeeze them firmly to remove as much moisture as possible. Add the onion and carrot and mix with your hands until well combined.

Mist a large skillet with cooking spray. Form about ½ cup of the potato mixture into a patty with your hands and carefully place it in the skillet. Fill the skillet with patties, leaving a couple of inches between them. Press gently with the back of a spatula to flatten the patties and cook until browned on the bottom, about 5 minutes. Turn, press with the back of the spatula again, and cook until browned on the other side, about 5 minutes.

Vegan **sour cream,** for serving

Applesauce, for serving

Transfer the pancakes to the baking sheet and put them in the oven to keep warm while you cook the remaining pancakes. Mist the skillet again before adding another batch. Serve garnished with parsley. Pass the vegan sour cream and applesauce at the table.

Per serving: 228 calories, 7 g protein, 1 g fat (0 g sat), 50 g carbs, 288 mg sodium, 110 mg calcium, 5 g fiber

Note: Analyzed with unsweetened almond milk. Analysis doesn't include parsley for garnish, and vegan sour cream and applesauce for serving.

Twice-baked potatoes are perennially popular and sure to be a hit. They're also substantial enough to serve as a main dish, perhaps with a large green salad on the side.

twice-baked POTATOES

4 large **russet potatoes,** scrubbed

4 tablespoons no-salt-added **vegetable broth,** plus more as needed

1 **yellow onion,** chopped

1 **red bell pepper,** chopped

1 cup chopped **mushrooms**

1 **green onion,** thinly sliced

¼ cup pitted **black olives,** chopped

¼ cup chopped fresh **parsley,** lightly packed

Position an oven rack in the center of the oven. Preheat the oven to 350 degrees F.

Prick each potato four or five times with a fork. Put the potatoes directly on the oven rack and bake for about 1 hour, until fork-tender. Let cool briefly. Leave the oven on.

Meanwhile, put 2 tablespoons of the broth in a medium saucepan, then add the yellow onion, bell pepper, mushrooms, and green onion. Cook over medium heat, stirring occasionally and adding more broth as needed to prevent sticking, until the vegetables are tender, about 15 minutes Remove from the heat and stir in the olives and parsley.

Increase the oven temperature to 400 degrees F.

When the potatoes are cool enough to handle, cut off a lengthwise piece of the top, about ½ inch deep. Coarsely chop the potato tops and put them in a medium bowl. Scoop out the flesh from the center of the potatoes and add it to the bowl. Be sure to leave enough flesh that the potatoes hold their shape, taking care not to pierce the skin.

Add the remaining 2 tablespoons of vegetable broth to the bowl and mash with a potato masher until creamy. Add more vegetable broth, 1 tablespoon at a time, if needed to achieve the desired consistency. Stir in the cooked vegetables. Spoon the mixture into the potato shells.

½ cup shredded vegan **mozzarella cheese**

Put the stuffed potatoes on a baking sheet and bake for 15 minutes. Top with the vegan cheese and bake for 5 to 10 minutes longer, until the potato skins are crisp and the cheese has melted.

Per serving: 381 calories, 10 g protein, 6 g fat (1 g sat), 75 g carbs, 288 mg sodium, 98 mg calcium, 11 g fiber
Note: Analyzed with Daiya mozzarella-style shreds.

TIPS FROM THE TRENCHES

"We both talked about healthier diets, but for a 'regular person' the idea of converting to veganism can be quite daunting. We started out by sampling vegetarian dishes at our favorite restaurants. Then we tried actual vegetarian restaurants. Once we knew what was involved, we began to cook vegan dishes for ourselves. It's been a team effort."

While this pilaf makes a tasty side dish, it's substantial enough to serve as a main course. If you do that, you might want to increase the amount of beans or add seitan or tempeh strips to up the heartiness quotient.

PEAS-AT-LAST pilaf

MAKES 4 SERVINGS

2 cups **water**

1 tablespoon **olive** or **sesame oil** (optional)

½ cup chopped **mushrooms,** any variety or a combination

½ cup thinly sliced **green onions**

½ cup chopped **yellow onion**

1 cup **long-grain brown rice** or **brown and wild rice blend**

1 cup no-salt-added cooked or canned **garbanzo** or **black beans,** drained and rinsed

½ cup shredded **carrot**

½ cup **corn kernels**

½ cup **petite peas**

½ cup finely chopped **zucchini**

2 tablespoons low-sodium **vegetable broth powder**

¼ teaspoon dried **chives**

¼ teaspoon dried **parsley**

¼ teaspoon dried **tarragon**

Salt

Ground **pepper**

Put ¼ cup of the water and the optional oil in a large saucepan, then add the mushrooms, green onions, and yellow onion. Cook over medium heat, stirring occasionally and adding more water as needed to prevent sticking, for 5 minutes.

Add the rice and stir until evenly coated. Stir in the remaining water and the beans, carrot, corn, peas, zucchini, and broth powder and bring to boil over high heat. Decrease the heat to low, cover, and cook for about 45 minutes, until all the liquid is absorbed and the rice is tender.

Remove from the heat and let sit covered for 5 minutes. Add the chives, parsley, and tarragon and fluff with a fork. Season with salt and pepper to taste.

Per serving: 367 calories, 13 g protein, 3 g fat (0.3 g sat), 73 g carbs, 70 mg sodium, 86 mg calcium, 8 g fiber

Note: Analysis doesn't include salt to taste.

Thousands of varieties of rice are grown worldwide. So, although arborio rice is traditional in risotto, why not shake things up and experiment with alternatives? Feel free to substitute other whole-grain rices in this recipe. Forbidden black rice or Bhutanese red rice would contribute wonderful flavor and texture, not to mention eye appeal.

AS-YOU-LIKE-IT risotto

See photo facing page 116.

MAKES 4 SERVINGS

3 cups **water,** plus more as needed

3 tablespoons low-sodium **vegetable broth powder**

1/2 cup **arborio** or **short-grain brown rice**

1/2 cup **brown and wild rice blend**

2 cups shelled fresh (see tip, page 55) or frozen **edamame**

1 small **yellow onion,** cut into half-moons

1 **red bell pepper,** cut into thin strips

1 large **carrot,** julienned

1 **green onion,** cut into thin strips

4 cloves **garlic,** finely chopped

1/2 cup shredded vegan **mozzarella cheese** (optional)

1/4 cup chopped fresh **basil,** lightly packed, or 4 teaspoons dried

Put 2 1/2 cups of the water and 2 1/2 tablespoons of the broth powder in a medium saucepan and stir to combine. Bring to a boil over high heat, then decrease the heat to low.

Put the arborio rice and brown and wild rice blend in large saucepan. Stir in 1/2 cup of the hot broth and cook over low heat, stirring often, until the rice has absorbed most of the broth. Add another 1/2 cup of the hot broth and continue to cook, stirring often, until the rice has absorbed most of the broth.

Repeat with three more additions of the broth; the entire process should take about 45 minutes. If the rice isn't tender after the entire 2 1/2 cups of broth have been added, continue cooking in the same way, adding water in 1/4-cup increments, until the rice is tender.

Bring a medium pot of water to a boil over high heat. Add the edamame. Return to a boil, decrease the heat to medium, and cook until tender, about 5 minutes. Drain well.

Put the remaining 1/2 cup of water and the remaining 1 1/2 teaspoons of broth powder in a medium skillet and stir to combine. Add the yellow onion, bell pepper, carrot, green onion, and garlic. Cook, stirring occasionally and adding more water as needed to prevent sticking, until the vegetables are tender, about 15 minutes.

Stir the vegetables, edamame, optional vegan cheese, and basil into the hot rice.

Per serving: 356 calories, 17 g protein, 6 g fat (1 g sat), 58 g carbs, 61 mg sodium, 9 mg calcium, 13 g fiber

With its combination of beans and rice, this side dish offers complete protein, so you can also serve it as a main dish. Even inveterate meat eaters will find it satisfying, especially if you include additional plant-based protein, such as vegan sausage or burger crumbles.

cajun RICE

2¾ cups **water,** plus more as needed

1 **onion,** finely chopped

4 cloves **garlic,** finely chopped

1 **green bell pepper,** finely chopped

1 **red bell pepper,** finely chopped

1 cup **long-grain brown rice**

2 teaspoons ground **cumin**

1 teaspoon **paprika**

½ teaspoon dried **thyme**

⅛ teaspoon **cayenne**

⅛ teaspoon **chili powder**

⅛ teaspoon ground **turmeric**

1 can (15 ounces) no-salt-added **kidney beans,** drained and rinsed

Put ½ cup of the water in a large saucepan, then add the onion and garlic. Cook over medium heat, stirring occasionally and adding water as needed to prevent sticking, until the onion is translucent, about 10 minutes.

Stir in 2 cups of the remaining water and the bell peppers, rice, cumin, paprika, thyme, cayenne, chili powder, and turmeric. Bring to a boil over high heat. Decrease the heat to low, cover, and cook for about 45 minutes, until the liquid is absorbed and the rice is tender. Remove from the heat and let sit covered for 5 minutes.

Put the beans and the remaining ¼ cup of water in a saucepan and cook over medium heat, stirring constantly, just until heated through, about 5 minutes. Drain well. Fluff the rice with a fork, add the beans, and continue to fluff with the fork until well combined.

Per serving: 295 calories, 13 g protein, 2 g fat (0.3 g sat), 60 g carbs, 29 mg sodium, 77 mg calcium, 15 g fiber

A buckwheat groat by any other name might sound more appealing, so I recommend that you use the alternative term "kasha," which simply means "roasted buckwheat groats." Kasha is the foundation of a beloved Jewish dish that incorporates bow-tie pasta, sautéed onion, and, unfortunately, often chicken or beef stock and egg. I loved kasha as a child, and this dish ranked high on the scale for comfort food, so I'm especially pleased to be able to share this vegan version with you.

KASHA AND **bows**

½ cup **water,** plus more as needed

1 tablespoon **Ener-G egg replacer**

1 cup **kasha** (see tips)

2 cups no-salt-added **vegetable broth**

8 ounces **portobello** or **cremini mushrooms,** thinly sliced

1 yellow **onion,** cut into thin rings

2 tablespoons reduced-sodium **soy sauce** (optional)

1 tablespoon **sunflower** or **olive oil** (optional)

1 cup whole-grain **bow-tie pasta**

Salt

2 tablespoons chopped fresh **parsley,** for garnish

Put ¼ cup of the water and the egg replacer in a small bowl and stir until well combined. Pour into a large nonstick skillet. Stir in the kasha and cook over medium heat, stirring constantly, until the kasha starts popping and smells toasty, about 3 minutes.

Stir in the vegetable broth and bring to a boil over high heat. Decrease the heat to low, cover, and cook until the kasha is tender, 15 to 20 minutes.

Meanwhile, put the remaining ¼ cup of water in a medium skillet, then add the mushrooms, onion, optional soy sauce, and optional oil. Cook over medium heat, stirring often and adding more water as needed to prevent sticking, until the onion and mushrooms are tender, about 15 minutes.

Bring a large pot of water to a boil over high heat. Stir in the pasta. Decrease the heat to medium-low, cover, and cook, stirring occasionally, until tender but firm. Drain well.

Add the pasta and the mushroom mixture to the kasha and stir gently until well combined. Remove from the heat and season with salt to taste. Serve garnished with the parsley.

Per serving: 262 calories, 11 g protein, 1 g fat (0 g sat), 53 g carbs, 13 mg sodium, 121 mg calcium, 8 g fiber

Note: Analysis doesn't include salt to taste and parsley for garnish.

TIPS

- Kasha (roasted buckwheat groats) can usually be found at well-stocked supermarkets in the international or natural food section.
- While the oil is optional in this recipe, including it helps the dish more closely emulate the traditional version.

This side dish is a perfect partner for Mexican food. To turn it into a meal, serve the beans over cooked whole grains or with cornbread on the side. The beans keep well and become even more flavorful after a day or two, so any leftovers can serve as the basis for a tasty, nutritious meal that will be a breeze to put together.

HOT 'N' spicy BEANS

1 cup dried **pinto beans,** soaked (see tips)

3 cups **water,** plus more if needed

1 large **onion,** chopped

1 **green bell pepper,** chopped

1 **red bell pepper,** chopped

2 ripe **Roma tomatoes,** chopped

1 **jalapeño chile,** seeded and chopped, plus more if desired

4 cloves **garlic,** chopped

2 teaspoons **chili powder**

1 teaspoon ground **cumin**

1 teaspoon **paprika**

Salt

Ground **pepper**

Drain the beans well, and then put them in a large pot with the water. Bring to a boil over high heat. Decrease the heat to low, cover, and cook, stirring occasionally, for about 1 hour.

Stir in the onion, bell peppers, tomatoes, chile, garlic, chili powder, cumin, and paprika. Cook, stirring occasionally and adding more water only if needed to prevent sticking, until the beans are very tender but not falling apart, about 1 hour longer. Season with salt and pepper to taste, and add more chile if you like.

Per serving: 231 calories, 13 g protein, 1 g fat (0.2 g sat), 44 g carbs, 33 mg sodium, 103 mg calcium, 13 g fiber

Note: Analysis doesn't include salt to taste.

TIPS

■ Soaking the beans prior to cooking will make them more digestible and speed their cooking time. Put the beans in a bowl or pot and add room temperature water to cover by several inches. Let soak for 8 to 12 hours.

■ For an even heartier dish, add chopped vegan kielbasa or vegan Italian sausage when adding the tomatoes.

Although this side dish is delish as is, feel free to give full rein to your creativity here, adding your favorite cooked vegetables or even minced or shredded raw vegetables. For a special treat, serve it with sauerkraut and rye bread on the side.

garlicky WHITE BEANS AND VEGGIE DOGS

1 can (15 ounces) no-salt-added **Great Northern** or other white beans, drained and rinsed

¼ cup **water**

½ cup **Garlicky Dijon Vinaigrette** (page 64)

6 ounces **vegan hot dogs,** cut into ½-inch-thick rounds

½ small **red onion,** cut into thin half-moons

½ cup chopped fresh flat-leaf **parsley,** lightly packed

Salt

Ground **pepper**

Put the beans and water in a saucepan and cook over medium heat, stirring constantly, just until heated through, about 5 minutes.

Drain well, then transfer to a medium bowl. Drizzle with the dressing and gently stir until the beans are evenly coated. Add the vegan hot dogs, onion, and parsley and stir to combine. Season with salt and pepper to taste. Serve warm or chilled.

Per serving: 157 calories, 13 g protein, 2 g fat (0 g sat), 24 g carbs, 467 mg sodium, 109 mg calcium, 8 g fiber

Note: Analysis doesn't include salt to taste.

TIPS FROM THE TRENCHES

"I've been in a bad marriage in the past. I'm so thankful to now have a husband who loves me and respects my choice to be vegan, even if he doesn't share that choice."

chapter nine

COMMON-GROUND DESSERTS

If all is fair in love and war, then winning nonvegans over with dessert may be totally justified—and possibly one of the more effective strategies available to you short of mind control. (But hmm, maybe it qualifies as mind control.) In all seriousness, though, keep in mind that "winning" may not be as important as celebrating what you have in common, and what better way to do that than with dessert? You've probably heard the relationship advice to never go to bed angry. Why not go one better and end the day on a sweet note?

If you can't please all of the people all of the time, perhaps you can please some of the people some of the time with this dessert—a bountiful selection of fresh fruits served over vegan ice cream. The ingredients aren't set in stone. You know your audience, so feel free to make substitutions or forgo any fruits that won't be winners.

rainbow FRUIT SUNDAES

1 **mango,** cut into cubes (see tip, page 47)

1 **orange, tangerine,** or **clementine,** peeled, sectioned, and seeded

1 fresh **peach,** sliced

½ cup fresh **blueberries**

12 **purple grapes,** halved

8 **strawberries,** halved

1 pint **vegan ice cream**

Unsweetened shredded dried **coconut** (optional)

Put the mango, orange, peach, blueberries, grapes, and strawberries in a medium bowl and stir gently to combine. Portion the vegan ice cream into serving bowls and top with the fruit. Sprinkle with coconut if desired. Serve immediately.

Per serving: 249 calories, 2 g protein, 8 g fat (7 g sat), 45 g carbs, 8 mg sodium, 33 mg calcium, 9 g fiber

Note: Analyzed with coconut milk-based vanilla ice cream.

TIPS FROM THE TRENCHES

"My wife rarely eats veggies, and most of the dishes she eats contain meat or dairy products. Nevertheless, she supports my vegan choices, and I love her even more for that."

This layered dessert is so attractive that you'll want to present it in glass vessels for maximum visual appeal.

FRUIT TRUCE **trifles**

2 cups **nondairy vanilla yogurt**

1 cup sliced fresh **strawberries**

1 cup fresh **blueberries**

1 cup fresh **raspberries**

1 cup fresh **blackberries**

¼ cup **granola**

4 teaspoons roasted sliced **almonds**

4 teaspoons unsweetened **cocoa powder**

4 large **strawberries,** for garnish

Distribute about ⅓ cup of the yogurt among four serving dishes, then top with half of the strawberries and blueberries. Distribute another ⅓ cup of the yogurt over the berries, then top with half of the raspberries and blackberries.

Repeat the layers: ⅓ cup of the yogurt, the remaining strawberries and blueberries, another ⅓ cup of the yogurt, and the remaining raspberries and blackberries.

Distribute the remaining ⅔ cup of yogurt over the berries, then scatter the granola over the top. Sprinkle with the almonds and then the cocoa powder. Top each serving with a strawberry.

Per serving: 234 calories, 8 g protein, 5 g fat (1 g sat), 39 g carbs, 52 mg sodium, 258 mg calcium, 10 g fiber

Note: Analyzed with vanilla soy yogurt.

This wonderful dessert is so simple yet so elegantly eye-catching. What's not to love about that? Although any vegan ice cream will work in this recipe, I highly recommend using one that's coconut-based for the richest flavor and creamiest texture. Many flavors are available. Choose one that complements strawberries.

strawberry DECADENCE

2 cups fresh **strawberries,** hulled

1 tablespoon **maple syrup** (optional)

1 pint vegan **coconut-based ice cream,** any flavor

1 cup raw or unsalted roasted **cashews**

2 tablespoons **vanilla extract**

4 teaspoons unsweetened **cocoa powder** (optional)

Put the strawberries and optional maple syrup in a blender or food processor and process until the strawberries are finely chopped but not mushy. Transfer to a small bowl and rinse out the blender. Put the vegan ice cream, cashews, and vanilla extract in the blender and process until smooth.

Distribute half of the ice cream mixture among four serving dishes. Top with half of the strawberry mixture. Repeat the layers, then sprinkle the cocoa powder over each serving if desired.

Per serving: 351 calories, 7 g protein, 20 g fat (9 g sat), 34 g carbs, 11 mg sodium, 30 mg calcium, 11 g fiber

Note: Analyzed with coconut milk-based vanilla ice cream.

This dessert is proof positive that deprivation is not a key ingredient in a vegan diet.

CHOCOLATE-MINT **parfaits**

2 frozen **bananas**

1½ cups vegan **chocolate chips**

2 teaspoons **vanilla extract**

½ teaspoon **mint extract**

8 leaves fresh **mint**

1 pint vegan **vanilla ice cream**

Put the bananas, 1 cup of the chocolate chips, and the vanilla extract, mint extract, and 4 of the mint leaves in a blender and process until smooth.

Distribute 1 cup of the vegan ice cream among 4 serving dishes. Top with half of the banana mixture. Repeat the layers, then sprinkle the remaining ½ cup of chocolate chips over the top. Serve immediately, garnished with the remaining mint leaves.

Per serving: 630 calories, 5 g protein, 32 g fat (22 g sat), 87 g carbs, 6 mg sodium, 3 mg calcium, 8 g fiber

Note: Analyzed with coconut milk-based vanilla ice cream.

CHOCOLATE-MINT SLUSHIES: This combination also makes a great slushy. Simply omit the vegan ice cream and the additional ½ cup chocolate chips. Once you've blended the banana mixture, pour it into glasses, garnish with the remaining mint leaves, and serve immediately.

This icy treat is much more healthful than expensive store-bought slushies.

RASPBERRY AND CHOCOLATE CHIP **slushies**

MAKES 4 SERVINGS

2 frozen **bananas**

1 cup frozen **raspberries**

1 cup **ice cubes**

¼ cup **water,** plus more if desired

1 cup vegan **chocolate chips**

Put the bananas, raspberries, ice, and water in a blender and process until smooth. Add more water if needed to achieve the desired consistency. Add the chocolate chips and process in short bursts, just until the chocolate chips are coarsely chopped. Serve immediately.

Per serving: 349 calories, 3 g protein, 16 g fat (10 g sat), 53 g carbs, 1 mg sodium, 11 mg calcium, 4 g fiber

TIPS FROM THE TRENCHES

"I occasionally cook salmon or eggs for my husband. Other than that, I only make vegan food. We recently decided that our holidays will be vegan, even though we're cooking for eight to ten people and only two of them are vegan."

When you serve this confection, people will know that you're really trying to win them over. Regardless of whether or not you succeed in that endeavor, everyone will be a winner when it comes time to eat these treats.

DATE NIGHT **truffles**

See photo facing page 117.

See photo facing page 117.

MAKES 6 SERVINGS

½ cup raw or unsalted roasted **almonds**

½ cup pitted **soft dates,** preferably medjool

½ cup **nondairy milk,** plus more if needed

2 tablespoons unsweetened **cocoa powder**

1 tablespoon **maple syrup** (optional)

½ cup **puffed wheat** or **rice cereal**

Put the almonds, dates, nondairy milk, cocoa powder, and optional maple syrup in a food processor and process until smooth, stopping to scrape down the work bowl a time or two. The mixture should be quite thick, but if it's too thick to process well, add more nondairy milk, 1 tablespoon at a time, as needed.

Scrape the mixture into large bowl. Add the cereal and stir gently with a rubber spatula until well combined.

Form the mixture into 1-inch balls. Put them on a plate, making sure they aren't touching, and cover with plastic wrap. Freeze until firm, at least 30 minutes. Let sit at room temperature to soften slightly before serving.

Per serving: 149 calories, 4 g protein, 5 g fat (1 g sat), 25 g carbs, 16 mg sodium, 84 mg calcium, 4 g fiber

Note: Analyzed with unsweetened almond milk.

CHOCOLATE-COATED DATE NIGHT TRUFFLES: For a hard chocolate shell, omit the cocoa powder and instead coat the balls in melted chocolate. Put 1 cup of vegan chocolate chips in a microwave-safe bowl and microwave in 30-second increments just until melted. The chocolate chips may retain their shape even when melted, so check by stirring with a fork. When the chocolate chips are mostly melted, stir until smooth. Line a plate with parchment paper. Dip each ball in the chocolate until evenly coated. Put the balls on the lined plate, making sure they aren't touching, and cover with a bowl. Freeze and serve as directed.

These lightning-fast tiny confections are sure to win over the hearts of anyone skeptical of vegan treats.

peanutty SNOWBALLS

½ cup unsalted roasted **peanuts**

4 pitted **soft dates,** preferably medjool

1 tablespoon creamy unsweetened **peanut butter**

6 tablespoons unsweetened shredded **dried coconut**

Put the peanuts, dates, and peanut butter in a food processor and process until well mixed but some texture remains.

Transfer to a bowl. Form into 6 balls. Put the balls on a plate and sprinkle with the coconut. Roll the balls around until evenly covered with the coconut. Serve immediately. Stored in a covered container in the refrigerator, these treats will keep for 1 week.

Per serving: 149 calories, 4 g protein, 9 g fat (4 g sat), 16 g carbs, 4 mg sodium, 17 mg calcium, 3 g fiber

This cinnamon-scented compote is a great dessert for a chilly autumn day. It's also healthful enough to serve for breakfast, perhaps as an accompaniment to granola. For a more decadent dessert, spoon the compote over vegan ice cream.

AUTUMN FRUIT compote

6 ripe **pears,** cut into large chunks

6 **apples,** cut into large chunks

Juice of 2 **oranges**

3 **cloves**

1 **cinnamon stick**

1 cup fresh or thawed frozen **raspberries**

1 tablespoon ground **cinnamon**

Put the pears, apples, orange juice, cloves, and cinnamon stick in a large pot. Bring to a boil over medium-high heat. Decrease the heat to low, cover, and cook, stirring occasionally, for about 1 hour, until the pears and apples are very soft and starting to break down.

Remove the cloves and cinnamon stick. Spoon the fruit into individual bowls. Top with the raspberries and sprinkle with the ground cinnamon. Break the cinnamon stick into chunks and use it as a garnish if you wish.

Per serving: 195 calories, 2 g protein, 1 g fat (0.1 g sat), 51 g carbs, 4 mg sodium, 45 mg calcium, 10 g fiber

This timeless dessert combines classic flavors that no one can resist.

banana SPLITS

4 ripe **bananas,** halved lengthwise

¼ cup vegan **chocolate syrup**

1 cup vanilla **nondairy yogurt** or **vegan ice cream**

½ cup chopped **walnuts**

¼ cup vegan **chocolate chips**

Put the bananas in serving dishes, 2 halves per dish. Drizzle each banana with 1 tablespoon of the chocolate syrup. Top each serving with ¼ cup of the vegan ice cream, then sprinkle with 2 tablespoons of the walnuts and 1 tablespoon of the chocolate chips. Serve immediately.

Per serving: 363 calories, 7 g protein, 15 g fat (4 g sat), 58 g carbs, 37 mg sodium, 113 mg calcium, 8 g fiber

Note: Analyzed with vanilla soy yogurt.

TIPS FROM THE TRENCHES

"I've been vegan for five years, and my family isn't. At home we eat only vegan, but if we go out for dinner, everyone has whatever they want. That mostly works out great. However, I won't kiss my hubby after he eats meat, so he usually skips it."

This cake is simplicity incarnate. One of the joys of vegan cooking is how unfussy recipes can be, as this scrumptious cake attests.

DATE AND NUT **cake**

MAKES 8 SERVINGS

1¼ cups whole wheat **flour**

1 teaspoon **baking soda**

1 cup chopped **soft dates,** preferably medjool

½ cup chopped **walnuts**

1 teaspoon **vanilla extract**

1 cup boiling **water**

Preheat the oven to 350 degrees F. Line an 8-inch square baking pan with parchment paper or mist it with cooking spray.

Put the flour and baking soda in a large bowl and stir to combine. Add the dates and walnuts and stir until evenly distributed.

Stir the vanilla extract into the water. Pour into the flour mixture and stir until well combined. Spread the mixture evenly in the lined pan and smooth the top with a rubber spatula.

Bake for 30 to 40 minutes, until a toothpick comes out clean. Serve warm or at room temperature.

Per serving: 232 calories, 5 g protein, 5 g fat (0.4 g sat), 47 g carbs, 168 mg sodium, 40 mg calcium, 5 g fiber

ONLINE RETAILERS

I t isn't a good idea to make a steady diet of processed foods. However, when first switching to a plant-based diet, many people find that including some vegan dairy and meat analogs can help them leap the hurdle. With time, these foods can be phased out in favor of whole foods, in the form that Mother Nature intended. You can probably find a wide variety of vegan alternatives at your local natural food store or a well-stocked supermarket. If not, here are some online sources.

The Dixie Diner's Club	dixiediner.com
The Mail Order Catalog for Healthy Eating	healthy-eating.com
May Wah	maywahnyc.com
Pangea	veganstore.com
Sophie's Kitchen	sophieskitchen.net/html/home.html
Vegan Essentials	veganessentials.com
VegeCyber	vegecyber.com
The Vegetarian Site	thevegetariansite.com

INDEX

Page references for recipe names and sidebars appear in *italics*.

Book Publishing Co.

books that educate, inspire, and empower

To find your favorite vegetarian products online, visit:

healthy-eating.com

Cookin' Crunk
Bianca Phillips
978-1-57067-268-2 • $19.95

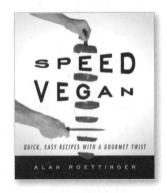

Speed Vegan
Alan Roettinger
978-1-57067-244-6 • $19.95

Eat Vegan on $4 a Day
Ellen Jaffe Jones
978-1-57067-257-6 • $14.95

Jazzy Vegetarian
Laura Theodore
978-1-57067-261-3 • $24.95

The 4 Ingredient Vegan
*Maribeth Abrams,
with Anne Dinshah*
978-1-57067-232-3 • $14.95

Grills Gone Vegan
Tamasin Noyes
978-1-57067-290-3 • $19.95

Purchase these health titles and cookbooks from your local bookstore or natural food store,
or you can buy them directly from:

Book Publishing Company • P.O. Box 99 • Summertown, TN 38483 • 1-800-695-2241

Please include $3.95 per book for shipping and handling.